MILESTONES

MILESTONES
On the Road Home

STEVE WARNER

WESTBOW
PRESS
A DIVISION OF THOMAS NELSON

Front Cover: Image Copyright Jens Ottoson, 2012;
Used under license from Shutterstock.com
All Bible quotations are from: The Holy Bible,
New International Version®, NIV® Copyright ©

WestBow Press books may be ordered through booksellers or by contacting:

WestBow Press
A Division of Thomas Nelson
1663 Liberty Drive
Bloomington, IN 47403
www.westbowpress.com
1-(866) 928-1240

ISBN: 978-1-4497-6337-4 (sc)
ISBN: 978-1-4497-6338-1 (hc)
ISBN: 978-1-4497-6336-7 (e)

Library of Congress Control Number: 2012916636

Printed in the United States of America

WestBow Press rev. date: 09/27/2012

"The path of the righteous is like the first gleam of dawn, shining ever brighter till the full light of day." Proverbs 4:18

Acknowledgments

Gratitude compels me to thank my wife, Mary, whose tolerance, sacrifice, encouragement, and practical assistance made this book possible. In addition, I must thank a particular friend whose love of language and heart for Jesus helped to make this work better, as well as the man who initially suggested the writings that became *Milestones*. No less importantly, deep appreciation flows to all the brothers and sisters in Christ who regularly motivate my scribbles and keep me moving forward on the road home. This book is a milestone in that journey.

Definition of **MILESTONE**: 1: a stone serving as a milepost. 2: a significant point in development.*

*by permission, *Merriam-Webster's Collegiate® Dictionary, 11*th *Edition,* © *2012,* by Merriam-Webster, Incorporated, www. Merriam-Webster.com.

Contents

Introduction

Intimacy does not come easily to us. We struggle to accept our responsibilities, or I should say we struggle not to. If we can find another to blame, including God, we will do so. So began the story with Adam's defensive statement, "It was this woman you gave me!" So the saga continues. Our own sense of self-sufficiency and our resulting refusal to ask for directions leaves us bewildered and far from home.

The ripples of our bewilderment reach the shores of our human relationships as well. Every year, I encounter relationships that have left the path of intimacy and never found their way back. Friends and lovers become baffled in the maze of human emotion. They, too, lose the road home.

As a counselor, I find it surprising that abandoned partners and friends usually believe it to be a sudden disaster. They had no clue. Sure, they engaged in minor skirmishes from time to time, just like everyone else. Contrary to appearances, love usually dies a slow death. The rubble of unresolved conflicts has buried their first love. Words spoken in anger that cut deep into the soul, apparent indifference to the physical and emotional struggles of a spouse, confused loyalty issues between a spouse and extended family members, unexplained desire for time away, and the emergence of a critical spirit—these, among other things, can bury love so deeply that people forget where to find it.

Worse yet, people reach a point of indifference. Their hearts become so wounded they grow numb. In a shock induced slowly over months or years, they let go of their partner's hand and simply walk away. In the rubble lie remnants of bright hopes and dreams of a future together, alongside promises and covenants long forgotten. Believing the situation hopeless, they walk into a grief that never completely goes away. They became one with another—now that "other" has gone. They started down the path leaning into one another, vowing always to support and guide. Now the marriage has ended; they may as well have lost the limbs on one side of their body.

Friends who once lit up in each other's presence now gaze blankly. Efforts to connect dwindle and eventually stop completely. The loss of a close friendship can be surprisingly devastating. Friends grow to depend on their companions for encouragement and exhortation, and a when a friendship suddenly ends, they are often very baffled. Without explanation, friends find no plan to redeem themselves; without communication and restoration, we discover no path home to loving friendship.

People can learn the skills necessary for resolving conflict in a healthy manner in about 15 minutes. Anyone who can drive a car or operate a television remote control has the mental wherewithal to learn these skills. So why do we see so many Christian marriages failing in our culture? Why do Christians sometimes feel as lonely as anyone else does?

Our relationship with God challenges us equally. If we cannot love people—whom we can *see*—then we are hard-pressed to love God, whom we cannot see. When life fails to live up to our expectations—when we grow weary fighting against the currents of our nature or when human relationships knock the wind out of us—we struggle to feel the presence of God. To the enlightened reader, the Bible tells God's story as he repeatedly extends himself to people, desiring relationship. It is the greatest mystery of all time, yet childlike in its simplicity. We can only find the home we long for in the intimate embrace of God. We find the only way home to it, as with the prodigal in the parable, by acknowledging our need for the Father. The narrow road requires us to sacrifice our pride in order to go through the gate.

This book entertains some thoughts, insights, and truths about these issues and offers some solutions to the age-old dilemmas that plague our relationships with God and one another. It hopes to challenge and expand our ideas of what it truly means to follow Jesus' example of living in grace and truth. And it posts some milestones to encourage you on your journey home to intimacy with God and others.

Ways to Use this Book

I designed the manuscript for *Milestones* with a wide variety of purposes in mind. For example, you might read it front to back, because the arrangement has a loose rhythm for that purpose. You may also peruse the contents like a menu and select a topic that speaks to you at a particular place along the way, reading thoughtfully, absorbing the reflection questions, praying deeply, and committing that milestone to memory. Should you spend a day on each, you will take (biblical sounding) 40 days to meditate on the material. If you choose to live with each milestone for about a week, the book will take you on a several-month's journey, and so on.

Most of us can benefit from being reminded, so I hope that some of you will live with the book, rereading parts you find especially helpful or challenging. Additionally, the content is particularly adaptable to devotional reading (public or private), using the reflection questions for discussions or introspection. Each individual's approach to prayer should be unique, so the suggested prayers are simply examples to get you going. In whatever manner you read it, this book wants to inspire you to take the biblical principles to heart, to live them out, to walk more fully in grace and truth.

Steve Warner

I am deeply appreciative that you have invested in *Milestones*. I pray that no matter how you decide to approach the writings, God uses them to encourage you on your journey to deeper relationship with him. Please bring someone along.

Fiddle Contest Rules

The fateful phrase jumped off the page: "Fiddle Contest, Sunday at Noon!" One Friday, on a whim, I picked up a paper while grabbing a burger. As I leafed through it, I came across a schedule for the Montrose County Fair. I did not suspect an adventure would follow.

You need to know a couple of things to understand this story. Years ago, I had a panic disorder that almost caused me to quit the seminary. The very thought of standing before a crowd would bring on debilitating heart palpitations, an inability to breathe, and a compelling urge to flee the scene. God used it to guide me into counseling as a profession and, over the last ten years or so, I have been in recovery, claiming my place on the platform by singing, playing, speaking, and acting. I have played fiddle just a few years—my church enduring the first faltering bow movements—and eventually have become a bit more confident as I stand behind the piano with my violin, blending in with the band.

I watch virtuoso violinists and weep, partly because of the beauty of the instrument unleashed, and partly because a barrier has stood between further competence and me. After all these years, the thought of standing center stage, playing my heart out, still seemed impossible from where I stood. What would happen if I had a panic attack? Not only could I be humiliated that day, but my reputation as a counselor would certainly fall suspect in the eyes of some in the community. On the other hand, if God would ever receive glory through this passion, I would have to break through the barrier.

So motivated, I go by the fairgrounds, ask a few questions, and read the poster:

Sign up starts at 10:30 on Sunday. Registration $12.

I start entertaining the idea. I picture a few fiddlers and several supportive family members. No big deal. What an opportunity to grow! Saturday morning I run through a few pieces and decide on a lovely Irish air. I will not compete with the seasoned players when it comes to speed, but I can play the air with lilt and passion. Besides, I want the accomplishment, not an award.

After singing at our church services on Sunday, I run over to the fair and give the people my $12. I see a couple hundred chairs there for an audience. *Optimistic,* I think.

When I come back after church, I see the chairs full of spectators, and the young division has started playing. Man, those kids can really play! Then I notice them playing *three* songs each!

I ask one of the volunteers about it, who replies, "Well, of course. Since the 1930s, fiddle contest rules have dictated that players will perform a waltz, a breakdown, and a song of choice."

My deer-in-the-headlights look and the blood rushing from my face elicit another response from him. "So if you can play a waltz, pick two more songs and you're good."

I call Mary on my cell phone and ask her to bring me some sheet music I've been practicing lately. She brings it, and I begin the process of elimination. While other fiddlers relax and get to a peaceful place, I scramble.

As I sit on the bench waiting my turn, I struggle to decide which three of five tunes I will play. The two performers ahead of me in the only adult division available prove themselves real pros, as in former winners and teachers! They dance through their tunes with the agility of speed skaters and the beauty of figure skaters. Meanwhile, there I sit on the bench, the titles of five simple songs scribbled on a napkin from my half-eaten lunch.

You have to understand. For years, I have had this very nightmare. In the dream, I stand in the wings, completely unprepared for the play, speech, or musical number. I usually wake up in a cold sweat before the inevitable agony of public humiliation. This fear has followed me all the days of my life.

As I sit there, I think, *I can just leave. I* am *a grown up, and no one can stop me!*

Then I look at the audience and see friends, supporters, and former clients waiting to hear me play. No, leaving evaporates as an option. I cannot disappoint my friends.

Then the enthusiastic announcement, "And here's Steve Warner from Montrose, Colorado!"

I look at the audience and the judges and say, "I'm here to provide a break from all this professionalism!"

The judges howl with laughter and I have won the audience. I explain I have never done this before, confessing my lack of preparation. I tell them I signed up on a whim and describe my ignorance of fiddle contest rules. I ask the head judge, "What's a breakdown?"

More laughter follows, but guess what? I feel no humiliation. I look the audience members in the eyes and say, "I'm here to get through this and to have the experience." Their enthusiastic applause surprises me.

I begin. The air (my waltz) floats across the room as if played by someone else. It comes across smooth and sweet, and I find myself swaying with it, carried to another place. I finish and the audience goes wild! They love it and surprisingly, it even sounds good to me. Then I follow with the breakdown (a familiar song in 4/4 time) played a little faster than normal, with only one slight hitch and a strong finish.

"Oh, yeah!" shouts a man in the crowd and again, wild applause. It echoes for David slaying Goliath and for the little train that could.

Something extraordinary just happened. The music came across okay, but they have heard better musicians for hours now. I think they're celebrating in seeing a 57-year-old man face his fears and conquer them!

For the last piece, I choose a very unusual Polish song in E minor with an odd European rhythm, precisely because I know they've heard nothing like it all day. I play it with passion and when I'm done the crowd goes wild again. When I walk the gauntlet to the back of the room, men and women rise to shake my hand and say things like, "That sounded great!"

As I sink onto the bench next to my wife she turns to me and says, "You have guts, baby!" I cherish the words every man wants to hear from his bride. Stunned, I have no idea what has just happened.

In the days that follow, I begin to get a perspective on the events. It has to do with growth, risk, and facing our fears. Every toddler falls, and if we continue to grow emotionally, we risk falling as well.

If you expect a Hollywood ending, you may be disappointed. We have no awards on the Warner mantle this week. However, I know I have won a victory, and no one can take it away from me.

I am grateful for many things: for a God who challenges me to face my fears and stands with his hand on my shoulder as I do so; for something in people that understands and roots for the underdog and recognizes what happens in situations like this; to have "Fiddle Contest" on my bucket list checked off!

> It is God who arms me with strength and makes
> my way perfect. (Psalm 18:32)

Reflections:

What has fear kept you from attempting?

God builds the potential for fear into us to keep us alive, so that we do not walk off cliff edges or into the jaws of hungry animals. What causes most of the fear in your life today?

The Bible frequently admonishes us to "fear not." What does this mean and how do we do this?

Jesus underwent extreme anxiety and stress in Gethsemane (Luke 22:44). How does this affect our interpretation of the "fear not" passages?

What fears are you willing to face if it means God could use you more fully?

Prayer:

Father, thank you for the depth and breadth of your love, for by it you called me into your family and held me in your loving arms. Living in a world broken since Eden's disobedience brings vulnerability to all kinds of dangers (catastrophes, illness, and evil deeds). Since the fall of man, bad things happen to good people. Beyond fearing those things, we sometimes fear disapproval and looking foolish.

Help me, Father, to change my perspective. Help me to see my life, and everything in it, more from your point of view. Everything I have belongs to you. Use it, or not, in your timing and not mine. Help me to remember that humility knows no humiliation and always gives an honest effort. You care about my willing heart. You could care less about my technical perfection, though you empower me to the best of my stage of development and beyond.

Help me to see you as the Father, sitting in the front row, grinning from ear to ear, so pleased with my honest efforts. When I do my best, it will fall short of perfect, but you listen to the music of the heart. When my efforts spring from love, you call them beautiful. Help me to sing on for your pleasure. In Jesus' name, Amen.

Milestone: I will face my fears in order to minister effectively in relationships with others.

Things Above

When I hear the testimonies of people who have come back from the verge of death, they impress me with how vividly they now live! They savor every flavor, drink in their experiences, and cherish each relationship. Almost universally, they talk about finding new purpose. They become keenly aware that they now live for a reason. They devote themselves to fulfilling their newfound destiny. Having faced the ultimate fear, they walk in a new realm of courage and faith.

The Apostle Paul wrote powerfully about Christ raising us to newness of life. The idea of God raising us with Christ carries with it so much meaning—rebirth following death to an old way of life. We now live on for a new purpose. Old goals and drives pass away, as if we have let go of one trapeze and now focus intently upon the next. The analogy holds true because it eliminates the option of holding on to both. We must choose one or the other. When it comes to the kingdom of this world or the Kingdom of God, we cannot have it both ways.

In Colossians 3, Paul encourages his readers, in light of the fact that God has raised them with Christ, to set their hearts on things above where Christ sits at the right hand of God. Paul employs imagery to help the church see Jesus seated in a place of honor, power, and authority above all, combatting heresies that placed Christ alongside other philosophies and religions. Seeing him in his place of rightful worship, all other things fade in relative glory and importance. He will not share his glory with other religions or philosophies. He will not share his worship in our lives with other priorities.

Imagine the earthly event that you see as most important—the Super Bowl, World Series, Academy Awards, Country Music Awards, or Indy 500—you name it. Then imagine that, at the height of drama at that event, the skies open up, a trumpet sounds, and Jesus steps onto the scene accompanied by all the saints who have ever lived! Which will grab people's attention more, do you think? No contest. The earth, with the best pyrotechnics and special effects people can muster, will pale in comparison to the presence of the resurrected Lord and heavenly hosts. So, why do we tend to live as though this earthly stuff matters most?

Years ago, I had a dream that I stood in line in a fun house, one of those venues designed to keep you off balance. You could not tell true vertical and horizontal, so you found yourself leaning a lot for support. This led to a lot of laughing and carrying on, so the line moved quite slowly. The operators had roped off the rooms of the fun house, but I became bored, so I got out of line (hard to believe, I know) and crossed one of the ropes. As I looked out the window of the upstairs room, I realized that the people ushered through the fun house exited in coffins! Those in charge entertained us "to death," making us victims of a conspiracy of distraction designed to keep us from thinking too much about our final destination and its meaning.

God wants us to wake one another up while we stand mindlessly in line. He means us for more than this, for the road we take has a destination. He designed us for eternal things, things above. Let us set our minds there. Where we store our treasure, there our hearts will also dwell (Matthew 6:21).

> Since, then, you have been raised with Christ, set your hearts on things above, where Christ is seated at the right hand of God. (Colossians 3:1)

Reflections:

If your mind could print out a history of your thoughts for the last week, where has it lived most? How has this influenced your emotions and actions?

How does the world attempt to keep your focus horizontal, fixed on things here below?

When you meditate on Christ's return, what do you feel? Fear? Shame? Joy? Peace? Why or why not? (Romans 8:1; I John 1:9)

What practical steps can you take to keep "things above" in the forefront of your life and relationships?

Prayer:

Father, images and noise bombard me these days, all designed to keep my focus on the material stuff and people who surround me here below. No wonder I long for what I do not have and covet my neighbors assets! It's not surprising that I become dissatisfied with what you provide for me when I think and live as if this life, in this world, matters most.

Help me, God. Please, give me eyes to see and ears to hear. Strip away the illusions of what matters. Reveal your plan, your majesty, and the glory of your appearing to me. Day by day, moment by moment, let me see your face and hear your voice. May that experience change me and have an impact on all that I touch. In Jesus' name and for his glory, Amen.

Milestone: I will train my eyes to look up so that my life priorities and relationships will match those of God's Kingdom.

Pure and Simple

Recently we picked up some seventies music CDs. After all these years, I felt as if I was hearing the words for the first time. I either had forgotten, or never knew, some of those lyrics were in those songs.

Have you had that experience when you hear a familiar passage of Scripture again, as if for the first time? Recently I heard a sermon on John 15, the passage about Christ as the Vine and us as the branches. As if for the first time, I heard the following phrase as a direct promise: "Remain in me and your fruit will be abundant."

A clearly marked signpost, the command is so simple and pure—so clear, direct, and typical of Jesus. So unlike us, really. "Pure and simple" does not always sell well in our age of high tech and complication-as-good. Frankly, our attitude sometimes sounds more like, "If just anyone can say it, present it, or get it, why care about it?" Jesus would care. As we fix our eyes on things above, we will care, too. Elitism cannot rule where simplicity reigns. In all honesty, we *like* elitism—as long as we fall among the elite. However, Jesus disrobed the elite on a consistent basis.

The religious rulers of Jesus' time complicated things beyond the ridiculous, but they missed the point: intimate relationship with

God. We would never do such a thing . . . maybe. If our theologies and books soar over the heads of the masses, and if our spiritual disciplines come from motivation to impress a God so holy that he has already pronounced our holiest human efforts as filthy rags, do we really look so different than the religious self-righteous of Jesus' day?

If we want abundant spiritual fruit, we will find the answer in the simple and profound principle, "abide in me." Some translate it as "remain in me." It means to take up residence, to find our home in him. One translation implies a deep organic relationship. I like that: living, growing, constantly in transition, and moving forward; bearing fruit of the Spirit, of the Kingdom, that nourishes others and self. Fruit comes from him, stacked both deep and wide. It stands the test of time and proves itself as his fruit by doing so. He promises all who abide in him abundant fruit!

Abiding reveals itself in relationship with him, by whatever means possible, as consistently as possible. It shows up in prayer, in listening for the voice of the Shepherd, in watching for his hand in the circumstances of the ordinary miracles of our days, and in digging deeply into his Word and finding truth about him there. As we do so, he challenges and transforms us over time, his Spirit in us and through us is unhindered. "Abiding" brings abundant fruit. Pure and simple.

> I am the vine; you are the branches. If a man
> remains in me and I in him, he will bear much fruit;
> apart from me you can do nothing. (John 15:5)

Reflections:

What kinds of distractions beckon you away from an abiding, faithful relationship with Christ? What motivates you to chase after these things?

When you think back to times when you seemed disconnected from the Spirit of Christ, how has the phrase "apart from me you can do nothing" manifested itself?

How might seeing "will bear much fruit" as a promise enhance your motivation to abide in him? How will "much fruit" bless your relationships with others?

Identify three things you can do to ensure that you abide in relationship with Jesus:

Prayer:

Father, thank you for revealing yourself in your Word in new ways all the time. Your promise that if I live in relationship with you I will bear much fruit both challenges and inspires me. Keep it at the forefront of my mind as I go through my days. Cause this truth to influence every choice and to shape each thought. Let "abide: bear abundant fruit" guide the values of my life. Let the fruit of your Spirit in my life draw others into deeper relationship with you. In Jesus' name and for his glory, Amen.

Milestone: I will live in relationship with Jesus so I will produce abundant fruit in relationships with others.

Sit Down and Shut Up!

I find my spiritual life, like many things, seems to run in cycles. At times—in those fleeting, shining moments—I perform like the MVP in my sphere of influence. Most of the time, I operate in the midst of the churning, turning team, doing my part to deliver the ball to the basket for the Kingdom of God. Other times, from my limited perspective, I sit on the bench, cheering on my team mates, praying for a chance to get on the court again.

During a recent bout of bench warming, I talked to God about what he wants from me next. The usual answer to this question runs something along the lines of "Show up and be faithful." On this particular day, however, the answer jarred and even bordered on what I would consider, well, rude—"Sit down and shut up!"

It occurs to me that the competitive (human) nature within me sometimes gets in the way of actual, meaningful relationship with God. I forget that he loves me, pure and simple, for reasons that have nothing to do with me and have everything to do with the loving nature of the Father. In this forgetful state, I seek to gain his approval, to stand out from the crowd, to become special—to become proud. The jarring mandate to "sit down and shut up" takes on new meaning, as an invitation to crawl into the loving lap of the Father and know stillness, to enjoy receiving his love because it pleases him to give it, and for no other reason.

I have come to love when the Spirit deals with me in strong conviction, silencing me with jarring love, shutting me up. At those times, I suspect that I come closest to seeing the very heart of the Father. In those moments, no doubt remains that he is God and I am not. In those moments, I taste home.

Abba, Father!

> Be still, and know that I am God; I will be exalted
> among the nations, I will be exalted in the earth.
> (Psalm 46:10)

Reflections:

What kinds of attitudes, activity and service make it easy for you to forget the Godhood of God?

Do you find yourself trying to earn the love of God? (See Romans 5:8.)

In what ways does your search for personal significance threaten to become your idol?

If you would sit down and listen, what would God want to say to you today?

Prayer:

Father, today I sit in silence, reflecting on all you have done to provide a way for me to enter your family, even when I wanted nothing to do with you. Shine a light on the ways I insult your gift by trying to buy it with my own efforts to prove my own significance, and then help me to lay those things aside, crawl onto your lap, and call you Father. I pray in the name of the One who paid the price so I could do so, Amen.

Milestone: I will put aside my efforts to prove my value in order to rest in the gift of God's extravagant love and learn to love others in the same way.

The Road Home

In a famous tale, two young innocents skipped into forbidden territory, dropping breadcrumbs behind them so they could find their way back. Of course, their plan had a fatal flaw. Forest foragers quickly ate the breadcrumbs, leaving them with no sense of direction. They became lost in a hostile land made worse by their encounter with a cannibalistic old woman. For those couples who have wandered haplessly into forbidden territory, we counselors serve in the role of guides to their destination.

Similarly, God has provided a road home to loving relationship with him. Paul's letter to the Romans includes Scripture's indictment and hope in parallel concepts: all have sinned and fallen short of the glory of God, but the gift of God is eternal life through Jesus Christ (3:23; 6:23). How seemingly hopeless we find the former statement and how utterly hopeful the latter! First, we must recognize that we have lost the way; having done so, Christ stands with open arms, eager to help us find our way. When we recognize that we have transgressed in the eyes of God, we need a plan of redemption. When we find that we have transgressed in the eyes of our spouse or friend, we will find our only hope in a plan of relationship redemption. We long for a way to make it right because we need a road home.

Just as there will be times to sit and be still, there are also times to get busy and to seek to heal relationships. Following this path home requires elements of repentance and grace. Repentance involves a recognition of the transgression (intentional or unintentional), an acknowledgment of the transgression, a seeking of forgiveness for the transgression, a change of mind about the behavior involved—and very significantly—a change in behavior.

Often this will involve a plan of correction, reminders, and eventual permanent change. This process of change sometimes requires patience that is similar to that of a parent watching a child learn a new skill. A toddler falls on his bottom more than he actually walks when making his first attempts. Far from scolding the child for doing so, most parents instinctively recognize falling as part of any learning process. This same attitude of acceptance and encouragement can help in any process of growth and change.

"Agape love" is the embodiment of relationship grace. When grace shows up in relationships, it hopes all things, believes all things, keeps no record of wrongs, never gives up, and always acts in the best interest of the other person. The true best interest of the other person involves, at times, speaking truth in love so that we may all grow up into the likeness of Christ (Ephesians 4:15). The notions of grace and agape do not contradict the concept of behavior change. We become members of God's family by faith in Christ; we demonstrate our love for him by obedience to his commands (John 14:21). When we love God, our behavior changes because we yearn to please him. We want to avoid offending him and learn to see people as he does. When we love others, we long to do what is good for them and we want to avoid hurting them.

The engagement of grace in this process involves forgiveness, just as God in Christ forgives us. When we step down from the throne of judgment, we know great relief in stepping out of our self-appointed roles as gods. We find ourselves side by side, fellow creatures in need of grace and seeking forgiveness, hope, and a way of redemption. Christ will meet us there, eager to illuminate our road home.

> Be kind and compassionate to one another, forgiving each other, just as in Christ God forgave you. (Ephesians 4:32)

Reflections:

When have you felt lost in a relationship, without hope for reconciliation? In retrospect, how did the relationship lose its way?

How does the grace of God make it possible for you to know him? (See Romans 3:23 and 6:23; Ephesians 2:8-10; John 3:16.)

How might full realization of God's grace for you affect your treatment of others? (See Ephesians 4:32; Luke 6:27-36; Matthew 18:21-35.)

Prayer:

Father, I admit that I have fallen short of your glory and do not deserve a relationship with you. I thank you for Jesus' sacrifice on my behalf, and I trust that what he has done covers me and provides me a way home to relationship with you, where my heart truly belongs.

I ask your Holy Spirit to have his way with me, to remodel me from the inside out. Give me my Father's eyes to see people and to love them as you do. Let your love and grace create a ripple effect in my sphere of influence that goes around the world and lasts for generations. In Jesus' name, Amen.

If you just prayed this for the first time asking Jesus to take control of your life, seek accountability and guidance in a local fellowship. Wherever you find yourself in your journey, ask Jesus daily to help you follow in his steps on the road home.

Milestone: I will repent, accept God's grace, and extend it to others.

Life and Death

A few times in the last couple of years, death seemed like a distinct possibility. A recent MRI of the brain comes to mind. To tell you the truth, thoughts of an early graduation to see Jesus face-to-face gave birth to comforting feelings. I became aware that *living* sometimes presents the bigger challenge.

Recently, I ran across a very familiar verse. In it, Paul boldly proclaims that for him, "to live is Christ and to die is gain." Many followers of Christ, me included, glibly quote this verse from time to time. As my walk home grows longer, I become increasingly aware of how far short I fall from truly owning this particular truth.

Okay, so I busy myself with Kingdom activities much of the time. I provide Christ-centered counseling as my career, I teach a Bible study in season, I sing and play music in his praise with a congregation, and my social networking site talks more about him than my activities of daily living. Nevertheless, what would change if, for me to live really *were* Christ?

The difference between walking in the Spirit and walking in the flesh is often subtle, and it frequently seems indistinguishable when viewed from the outside. In fact, I can make the shift in a millisecond, overlooking the change for hours or even days. This painful admission places me in good company, I suspect. In one moment, we make it all about Jesus; in the next, often without a conscious decision, we make it all about us.

I have often thought that the difference between the natural man (apart from God) and the spiritual man (filled with God's Spirit and seeking communion with him) manifests in this very struggle. If Christ and my life became inseparable, I think I would not so blindly shift into life in the flesh, the self. If I roll into my pillow and cut off my own air supply, I really notice that quickly. If I miss a meal, the pangs get my attention right away. But if I turn away from Jesus, I become as the donkey at the triumphal entry: I need to remember that the praises that surround me do not belong to me.

In truth, I find conviction strangely comforting. God chastens every son he loves, and I see it as a good thing to have this frequent evidence that I belong to him. The Spirit's work in remodeling my heart demonstrates the kindness and patience of the Father. Far from discouraged, I find great security in his persistent hammering and demolition within me. He loves me more than I can comprehend just as I am and far too much to leave me this way. I pray for me and for you that before we experience "to die is gain," we can truly say "to live is Christ!"

> For to me, to live is Christ and to die is gain.
> (Philippians 1:21)

Reflections:

Have you had any narrow escapes when you thought you might not make it? Did you feel peace, terror, or something else? From where did these feelings arise?

Which challenges you most: "to live is Christ" or "to die is gain"? Please explain your answer.

What did Paul refer to when he said, "to live is Christ"? Truthfully, how does this match with your daily life? How might living in this truth affect your relationships with people?

How can you bring your day-to-day walk into line with Paul's confident statement that his life is Christ? What stops you?

Prayer:

Father, honestly, Paul's words "to live is Christ, to die is gain" greatly test me. How easily my life becomes just that: *my* life. How I cling to the life in this body, wanting what is familiar and fearing the unknown! Yet when I read Paul's words, I know instinctively that you desire to give me this peace and confidence in my daily experience.

Help me to let go of what I believe I own, realizing that you have bought me at a great price. Each day, each moment, and each breath belong to Christ. As I learn to give them to Jesus, fill me with the peace and confidence that comes from knowing I have placed them in the very best hands possible. Let this motivate me to reach out to others and love them into your Kingdom. In Jesus' name and for his glory, Amen.

Milestone: I will find peace in knowing my life and eternity are safe in Christ as I reach out to others on the road home.

Not Earthly Things

Some of my fondest memories took place in a pastor's study in Topeka, Kansas. There, a good friend, for whom to live really *is* Christ—gave of his time and fanned a flame in me for the love of language, specifically the Greek language of the New Testament. I was finding my own way back to the path of God at the time through a series of quiet encounters that changed my life for the better. My eyes moved from the carnal lifestyle I adopted in fraternity days, as I began to focus on things above.

One of the concepts I learned from my friend was that the *Koine* Greek versions of the New Testament lacked the punctuation marks today's readers have come to rely on for emphasis. When a writer wanted to exclaim a point, he repeated it. When he wanted to exclaim it and carry it forward, he repeated it and added another point. Paul did this when writing Colossians 3:2. Today's reader feels tempted to pass over it, thinking perhaps Paul was being repetitious, and we have already heard this point. Rather, Paul says that his point is crucial, central to the Christian way of life, and bears repeating. "Don't miss this!" he exclaims from between the lines. In an informal letter written today, we bold it, write in all caps, and top it off with an exclamation mark:

SET YOUR MINDS ON THINGS ABOVE, NOT ON EARTHLY THINGS!

The church needed this teaching on multiple levels. His readers entangled their beliefs in a web of human philosophies that competed with the message of Christ as supposed equals. As they set their minds on such things, they became vulnerable to going astray, away from the pure gospel of salvation by faith in Jesus Christ that Paul had entrusted to them, at risk to his own life. A strong theme in his letter to their church, clearly this motivated his writing these words to them now. He also wrote to address their ongoing battle with human nature (I want what I want when I want it), and spiritual shortsightedness (this world is what matters; live for today). For all these reasons, Paul felt the need to impress upon them his message: keep your eyes upon Jesus; forget everything else.

Today the Church, especially in western civilization, faces many of the same issues. In our well-intentioned efforts to "converse" with everyone, we run the risk of implying to a new generation the idea of Jesus' teachings as just another philosophy to set on the shelf alongside others. Paul knew no such mindset, and when he spoke to other believers, he had no tolerance for such teachings. He insisted that Christ reigns as Lord of all or Lord of nothing at all. In verse one he has just placed Jesus in his rightful position, at the right hand of the Father in heaven. He makes room for no one else there.

Many other earthly things compete for our attention and worship. I challenge you to ask the Holy Spirit to show you, over the next few weeks, whatever things compete with Jesus in your heart. He will surprise and reward you in the process. He may illuminate for you not only the obvious things—big TVs, cars, money, trips, and home-remodeling projects—but also the good things, such as ministries and people that have slipped into his place. In this process, I have realized that the things I worry about have often slid onto the throne that should belong to Christ.

Remember that, what the Spirit shows the believer, he shows for healing, not condemnation. I encourage you to welcome his touch in this process. He has nothing but your best interest at heart.

In this beautiful passage, Paul interweaves themes of the majesty of Jesus above all else, and the peace that comes from remembering this. I sincerely pray that you will not just glance at these verses, but that you welcome God's Word deep within your spirit to have his way there. In so doing, you will truly set your mind on things above, where Christ sits at the right hand of God. You will not want anything else.

> Set your mind on things above, not on earthly things. (Colossians 3:2)

Reflections:

What kinds of things, issues, or people compete with Jesus for his place on the throne of your heart?

What emptiness do you hope to fill with these things? How does that work for you?

If you look at all of these things in a pile on one hand, and Jesus' love and peace on the other, what makes the choice so difficult?

What steps will you take to put these things in their rightful place and Jesus in his?

Prayer:

Father, like the Israelites of old, I tend to drift into idolatry. Truthfully, I seldom set out to worship idols. I would see that temptation clearly and avoid it. More often, I tend to let things creep slowly and subtly onto the throne of my heart until they edge out Jesus.

Father, you have placed him at your right hand. Help me to see him there. Let me entertain no competing ideologies of philosophies as his equals. Cause me to see clearly what these lack, and let your Spirit call me back to "the way, the truth, and the life."

I willingly lay down every idol. Help me to express gratitude for your good gifts. No longer will I confuse the gift with the Giver. If any of these things fall outside your will for me, I will count them as nothing. I will cast them aside and forget about them so that I can always remember you. Let the priority of relationship with you touch each relationship with others. In Jesus' name and for his glory, Amen.

Milestone: As the Spirit opens my eyes to the idols I have collected, I lay them down and bow with my brothers and sisters at the feet of Jesus.

The Whisper

"Where has God gone? I cry out to him and hear no answer! My prayers bounce off the ceiling! Just when I need him the most, he remains aloof!"

Cries of lamentation challenge my ability to respond as a Christian counselor more than most. The scholar in me wants to correct the faulty theology—that God is aloof—but the phrase "God is omnipresent" falls on deaf ears at such times. The therapist in me wants to affirm the emotional state of the clients, because earthly concerns have clouded their ability to see things above right then. Even though I know that God is available when they're ready for him, that doesn't *feel* true to them. The challenge for me is to meet my clients where they are at that moment, while remaining biblically grounded.

The importance of timing carries more importance in my field of healing broken hearts than in most areas of life. As friends and lovers, we can take a lesson from that principle. A friend calls, and tells us his sibling has died at 30 years of age. Glibly quoting "All things work for the good of those who love God" will not help right then. A spouse recounts the tale of her day, ridden with misunderstanding and betrayal. Advice will not assist her at that point.

When people shuffle into my office, eyes lowered and red from a state of no more tears to cry, advice and pat answers fall among the least helpful things I can offer them. First, they need me to hear them. They need understanding; they need another human heart to break a little over their loss, their disillusionment, their sorrow.

Over half the Psalms lament the state of the writer, telling tales of woe. "Many are those who gather around me . . ." speaks not of those gathering with helpful intentions. "How long, oh Lord . . ." does not question undying blessing. No, these songs, poems, and letters express confusion in the maze of human emotion as it interfaces with theology. They cry out as if to say, "You said you'd never leave me! Well, where have you gone! You promised you had my back! So why does my backside seem so exposed and bloody? I feel that you have let me down! How much longer do you expect me to just hang out here, vulnerable to the enemies of spirit, heart, life, and limb?"

If this sounds irreverent to you, read the Psalms anew, looking for the anguish of faith put to the test. You will find it there. As you read between the lines, look, if you will, for the great Listener. He loves with patience, kindness and long-suffering. He never gives up, never lets go, and he finishes what he has started. Eventually, most of these Psalms "ascend" to a perspective of faith. However, why not just start and end on a positive note? Why did the Holy Spirit, still cloaked behind a veil in the Holy of Holies, open the hearts of the authors to include such cries of anguish?

Such angst gives us glimpses of emotional and spiritual authenticity before God. He gave his only Son to redeem our right to such relationship with him. Mystery of mysteries, he longs for this authenticity from you and me. He wants us to express our feelings to him from open, unguarded hearts. He can handle it; he can redeem it. He can listen, empathizing as a high priest who has been tempted in every way. Just at the right moment, and not a moment too soon, he will whisper just the right word to our hearts: no lecture, no theological discourse on faith. Our hearts will bear witness to him as, after all, trustworthy.

Sometimes the whisper comes from the still depths of our own hearts. Sometimes it will be a Scripture recalled, maybe even Romans 8:28, but at the right time. Sometimes the whisper appears as a song on the radio, a call from a friend who has had us on his mind, or the gentle nurturing touch of our lover.

When the time is right, the wave of lamentation washes back out, lost in the depths once more. We change forever, and for the better, for our honesty before God. He smiles. He knew all along that we would find the path home.

> How long, O LORD? Will you forget me forever?
> How long will you hide your face from me?
> (Psalm 13:1)

> My God, my God, why have you forsaken me?
> (Psalm 22:1a; Mark 15:34b)

And we know that in all things God works for the good of those who love him, who have been called according to his purpose. (Romans 8:28)

. . . Then a great and powerful wind tore the mountains apart and shattered the rocks before the LORD, but the LORD was not in the wind. After the wind there was an earthquake, but the LORD was not in the earthquake. After the earthquake came a fire, but the LORD was not in the fire. And after the fire came a gentle whisper. When Elijah heard it, he pulled his cloak over his face and went out and stood at the mouth of the cave . . . . (I Kings 19:11-13)

When have you felt God to be distant?

When have you struggled to help another when they felt the absence of God? How did you respond? What resulted?

When your emotions tell you one thing, and the promises of Scripture tell you another, which is telling you the truth?

How can you comfort yourself and others in a way that honors feelings without compromising biblical truth?

Prayer:

Father, you have promised that you will never leave me or forsake me. In your flawless nature, I find only truth and faithfulness to your promises, especially the ones that involve your children. Thank you for being trustworthy.

In my walk through this broken world, I encounter times when it seems as if you have left me. It sometimes appears as if you stand aside, indifferently. Job, David and Jesus all faced this feeling. When I walk through such times, help me to express the emotions to you in deep relationship while anchored in the absolute truth that you will never abandon me.

Help me to remember these things as I seek to offer comfort. Grant me an extraordinary measure of the fruit of your Spirit: love, joy, peace, patience, kindness, goodness, faithfulness, gentleness, and self-control. As these things flow from you through me, may others realize your presence. May they know a taste of your caring as they see mine. In Jesus' name and for his sake, Amen.

Milestone: As I anchor myself in the trustworthy nature of God, I find and share a peace that surpasses my emotions.

Faithfulness

The fickle nature of the public amazes me. Today's sport celebrity becomes tomorrow's loser. The mega-star of yesterday becomes today's has-been. People spend many thousands of dollars to replace fully functional sinks, appliances, and countertops because magazines sell us what we "need" to remain trendy. Today's technology will lose ground and will "need" replacement by next year. We have become a nation with attention-deficit problems, needing constant excitement and stimulation. We desire something new to covet and clutch every few minutes. We exchange emotional stimulation for true faithfulness.

The results of this tendency reach far into our relationships as shown through our boredom with real conversation. I recently attended a dinner gathering at the home of some Godly people. Their adult children sat around the table using their phones to text and surf during dinner. Their attention divided, no real communication occurred.

I talk with couples every day who have become bored with the sameness of their marital relationships. The need for constant change has affected people's ability to sustain long-term intimate relationships. A man thinks, "Maybe the woman at work who really 'gets me' would appreciate me more." People abandon marital vows in favor of a new model.

Similarly, we view solid, sustainable doctrine as old, tired, and boring. Like the children of Israel who cried for meat in the wilderness, we have become bored with the manna of the Word. We seek new and exciting varieties of teaching. It becomes attractive to seek "new" theologies that are, in reality, old lies repackaged for a new generation.

We have lost our contentment. We have lost our faithfulness. We have abandoned springs of living water and have built our own wells, filling them with the muck of this world, and then bemoaning our unending thirst. Becoming bored with our Husband—God in the person of Jesus Christ—we entertain thoughts of infidelity. Some of us have walked away from him completely. Having left behind the transitional stages of loss of contentment and loss of faithfulness, we ourselves have become lost.

Each day, we stand at a crossroads. One heavily travelled path leads where the world will take us, and our values, marriages, faith, and families will suffer the impact as we clutch at worthless trinkets. The other less-travelled path leads home—to contentment, to faithfulness, and to God. He watches from afar, eager to meet us on the way home. Choose your path wisely.

> What good will it be for a man if he gains the whole world, yet forfeits his soul? (Matthew 16:26)

Reflections:

What distracts you from Jesus and his unchanging truths?

How does restlessness in your spirit affect your relationships with God and with others?

What steps will you take to keep yourself faithful to him and to one another?

Prayer:

Father, I confess the restlessness of my heart. I chase the next shiny object, oblivious to the fact that it takes me farther from you and farther from meaningful relationship with people. Help me to breathe deeply and fix my eyes upon Jesus. The lover of my soul, you remain faithful day after day, waiting for me to understand fully the depths of your riches for us: spiritual, emotional, and eternal. You long for me to love others into relationship with you. Your truths remain the same, century after century. I have no reason to keep searching. As I follow you, I find myself, faithfully, on the road to home. Keep me there, I pray, in Jesus' name, Amen.

Milestone: As I bring others along, I embrace the truth that the surest way to reach a destination is to remain, faithfully, on the pathway to it.

Paving the Way

Colorado locals know all too well that when we have lost our way in the wilderness, nothing matters so much as our desire to find the path again, to get back on track. The overwhelming sense of disorientation and the sinking loss of bearings drive us to locate familiar territory once more. We are eager to do whatever it takes to alleviate the hopelessness that accompanies losing our way. In the same vein, when we stray from the path of relationship, we need to find solid footing to find faith in God or others once more.

We must pave the road to intimacy with solid changes. People proclaim their willingness to do anything as they watch their now-indifferent mate walking away. When the words, "I'll do what I have to," spring forth for dramatic effect, they ring hollow after a time. Yet when words express a true desire of the heart, they herald hope to mend the relationship. If only the indifferent partner will stay long enough to see the words put into actions. These stones pave the path home to loving relationships of all kinds.

First, we need to listen, to hear clearly what we have done (or not done) to wound our partner or friend. An error in thinking that I encounter as a counselor is what I call a "fallacy of intentions."

In other words, if I did not *intend* to hurt you, you should not feel hurt. The husband who works long hours to the detriment of his marriage exemplifies a good intention that can fatally wound a relationship. The fact that someone feels hurt stands on its own. We need to show humility and willingness to listen to the pain we have caused without defending our egos and flexing the muscles of "being right." In time, we can explain that love drove some of our decisions while owning our mistakes. However, *listen first!* In so doing, we accomplish two things: we understand the point of view of our partner as we exhibit compassion for them. We also help them reduce their anger by venting what smolders inside them. If you think this sounds like psychology and not very Christian, read the Psalms anew, looking for the heart of the Father who patiently listens while the writer laments his way back into fellowship.

Next, we need to acknowledge that we have hurt someone we love and apologize for it. An apology simply states that we recognize that our actions or choices have become a source of pain to the other person. For example, saying, "I'm sorry you were hurt by that," implies the reason the person was hurt lies with *them* and not with the one who made the offending comment. Such a statement might well hint that the other person appears too sensitive and that you've done nothing wrong. A truer apology would sound like, "I'm sorry that something I did caused you pain and doubt in our relationship."

Frequently, we overlook the need to seek forgiveness. If we do not ask for it, forgiveness can fall by the wayside, and the hurt can go into the pile of resentments unleashed as ammunition later. Forgiveness requires conscious decisions. You read it right: that's a plural—*decisions*. When we forgive, we need to decide to give up our options to punish each other for transgressions, stop the mental replays of the movies in our head regarding the transgression, and give the person to God the Holy Spirit to bring about any needed change of heart and behavior. When we ask for forgiveness, we make these decisions conscious in the minds of the other. Of course, the fact that we ask does not require the other person immediately to forgive us. Some wounds take time to heal, and we need respectfully to grant that time.

As we see our actions through the eyes and heart of our partner, we may begin to change our minds about what we do or how we do it. To touch back on the example of working hard, many men and women do it precisely because they do love their families. Yet the absence from the home of a mate or a parent over a long period can cause loneliness, pain and eventual indifference. If I become aware that my actions cause pain to my spouse, my friend, or my God, I change my mind about the meanings of my actions. A favorite proverb states that as a man thinks, so will he be. Therefore, a true change of mind would bring about change in behavior.

What would result if we stop here? Perhaps you have come across a person who gracefully accepts your feedback that you find some of their actions painful, who verbalizes empathy for your point of view, who acknowledges that they could/should do things differently—but nothing changes. Eventually, the maxim, "Actions speak louder than words," wins out. Jesus asserted,

"The one who loves me is the one who keeps my commands." Eventually, even gracious Jesus expects us to walk the talk and in human relationships, the same rings true. If I say the words "I'm sorry" but continue my old behaviors, ultimately the other person will see my words as empty or untruthful. If I say one thing and do another, others will believe my actions and not my words.

Therefore, as a crucial step of paving the way home, I need to dedicate myself to alter what I do to bring it in line with what I say. Just as the Bible calls faith without actions "dead," relationships without actions eventually die. When we love someone, we need to find out what actions, words, or deeds translate into love in their spirit and commit to doing those things on a regular basis. People vary vastly in their interpretations of actions, words, and gestures as evidenced by entire books written on the subject of the languages of love. Spend some time talking to your partner about their needs, and do everything in your power to do those things.

We need to extend grace to one another, especially in the process of change. We do not scream at toddlers who fall on their bottoms, skiers on the bunny slopes, or people learning new skills in sports or music, so we need to offer kind understanding as our partner or friend takes faltering steps in the right direction on the road home.

> Do nothing out of selfish ambition or vain conceit, but in humility consider others better than yourselves. Each of you should look not only to your own interests, but also to the interests of others. (Philippians 2:3-4)

Reflections:

What tendencies make it difficult for you to simply listen to your partner, friend, or child? What would improve in your relationships if you developed the skills of a good listener?

What makes apologizing so difficult? Does an apology always mean that you have done wrong? Why do you think so, or not?

Do you see forgiveness as the same as excusing the other person's behavior? What must one do to forgive another?

Does repentance go beyond saying "sorry"? If so, how does it?

How will you weave grace into the process of repentance, forgiveness, and change? (See Colossians 3:13; I John 1:9.)

Prayer:

Father, I thank you for your grace, forgiveness, and patience with me. I am so grateful that you do not expect perfection of me. Thank you for your Spirit, who keeps me moving forward and making progress. Help me to see the people in my life as you see me—imperfect yet forgiven, each one priceless and worth dying for. Help me to give away gracious forgiveness just as you have forgiven me in Christ. Amen.

Milestone: I will learn to apologize and to forgive others as I grow in understanding God's grace for me.

Anger and Love

It comes up daily in counseling sessions. Those we let the deepest into our hearts can cause the most anger in us, and we tend to unleash that anger most freely on those closest to us.

It should come as no surprise that in order to mature emotionally and spiritually, we must choose connection over isolation. When we begin to feel close to people and they fail to live up to our expectations (some legitimate), we encounter decisions about whether to move into relationship or away from it. Our culture makes it easy to walk away. If this choice becomes a lifestyle, eventually we may lose our way and find ourselves in hopeless isolation.

Ephesians 4 states, "In your anger, do not sin." It clearly acknowledges that anger does occur, without calling anger itself sinful or necessarily incompatible with love. In the pages of the Bible, YHWH loves Israel with a passionate and sometimes angry love. The book of Hebrews states that he (a literal translation) "skins alive every son he loves." Jesus' transparent frustration with his closest followers, whom he deeply loved, gives us a picture of anger and love connected.

I see anger as a God-given emotion, like any other, with a purpose and a potential abuse. Jesus' anger in the temple led him to overturn tables as the self-righteous and the arrogant took advantage of the poor and disenfranchised. When we see injustice today—especially in the family of God—anger, in my opinion, emerges as an appropriate Christ-like response. When we seem disrespected or unloved (basic emotional needs in marriage and other intimate relationships, e.g., Ephesians 5), anger becomes a natural response. God endorses anger *for the right reasons*, and it's good if used *as constructive energy*. God gave us anger to use as just that—energy to drive us to right the wrong.

In close personal relationship, this may follow a simple formula: Facts (a brief non-inflammatory description of the problem), Feelings (how I feel about the situation), and Fair Request (we offer a possible solution). We do this privately and one on one, per Matthew 18:15. Of course, this assumes that our hearts truly desire to solve the problem, not to perpetuate it, retaliate, or seek personal vindication. We do not own rights to vindication. That belongs to God.

When we see injustice in the Church, we should go to the person responsible, offer our observation, and suggest a solution. We should desire reconciliation to restore them gently (Galatians 6:1). This will not always seem possible, perhaps due to confidentiality constraints, for example. In those cases especially, I have found it extremely helpful to follow the example of the psalmists, I write letters to God about my frustration and anger, asking him to rectify the situation and deal with each person as only he can do. As I do this, anger subsides and peace rises.

When I let the sun go down on my anger—when I nurture it and keep the fire stoked, I "give the devil a foothold" (Ephesians 4:26-27). This gives room for my walk to leave the path of God's will and grieves the work of the Spirit in me and through me. It can turn into passive-aggressive behaviors such as gossip (sharing other people's information, whether true or not, see the chapter titled "Why the Drama"), aggressive behaviors as brawling, or into verbal assault and other sins of the tongue so vividly described in the book of James.

Unfortunately, even if we do everything right, we cannot mend all relationships. People make their own choices in spite of our eloquent fair requests. Some people seem virtually incapable of owning responsibility and making meaningful changes. Then decisions face us about degrees of involvement in those relationships. There are people in my life who do not have access all the way into my heart, but I do not exclude them from it entirely. This is a personal conviction; I do not call it truth, necessarily.

God created us in his image, and he sometimes exhibits anger. We have to sort out if our anger comes from righteous motives (as opposed to self-centered) and we need to use it constructively, to right the wrongs within our control or to pray to the One who can. Using our God-given anger for good becomes another portion of the map to help one another on the journey home.

> In your anger do not sin. Do not let the sun go
> down while you are still angry, and do not give
> the devil a foothold. (Ephesians 4:26-27)

Reflections:

What kinds of situations tend to trigger your anger? Do you think you feel anger more often, less often, or about the same as others? Can you think of someone you admire for the way they handle conflict situations?

How can we know if our anger comes from righteous or self-centered motives? (See James 3:13-4:12.)

Scriptures teach us how to address situations when someone sins against us. (See Matthew 18:15-17; Galatians 6:1.) How easy do you find it to handle things this way? What makes it difficult?

Ultimately, we need to put our anger to rest. Do you struggle with forgiving someone who has wronged you? What did Jesus teach about forgiveness? (See Matthew 6:12; Luke 6:27-36.)

What issues do you need to take a stand on for Christ's sake? What steps do you need to take to forgive someone who has wronged you?

Prayer:

Father, thank you for creating me in your image. You have given me the potential for love, passion, anger, and mercy. Help me to keep in mind that while created like you, I am *not* you. When I am angry, let me look at my own heart first. When my anger comes from selfishness, help me to take it to you and ask you to remove it, giving me patience and kindness instead.

When my anger is righteous, on behalf of the best interest of others and the gospel of Christ, help me to deal with people constructively, seeking solutions based in the truth of your Word. Let me make it my goal to "restore them gently." Help me to walk away from such situations, sensing your pleasure because I offered mercy and helpfulness. Keep me from stumbling on my own pride. Finally, help me to change the things I can, accept the things I cannot, and—mostly—to know the difference. I ask these things in Jesus' name and for his glory, Amen.

Milestone: With God's help, I learn when and how to use my anger, and when and how to let it go.

Hidden with Christ

If I pick up a letter written to someone else and peer into its secrets, I will know a little about its contents, but my understanding will lack fullness because I do not know the people, the circumstances of the writing, or the exact nature of the relationship. My comprehension is no broader or deeper than my knowledge of the context. Even my anger often arises from misunderstanding the full backdrop to actions and words. The more profound my understanding of context, the greater will be my insight.

Paul reminded the church in Colossae:

> For you died, and your life is now hidden with
> Christ in God. (Colossians 3:3)

Taken out of context, this verse can lead to some confusion. However, Paul has just laid a foundation: the believing readers need to see themselves as raised with Christ and need to set their hearts on things above, where Christ sits at the right hand of God (vs. 1). In light of this, Paul emphatically repeats, they need to set their minds on things above, not the things of this world (vs. 2). Because of the realities just mentioned, they should see themselves as dead to this world, and to the tyranny of the flesh, remembering that God hides their new life with Christ.

This hiddenness includes a sense of concealment and security. It carries meanings of invisibility (to those in the world) and safety. We hide ourselves in him. How do we reconcile the word *hidden* with Jesus' insistence that the life of a true believer will be like a city on a hill and a lamp on a stand, impossible to hide in a dark world? I believe the truths of these two teachings can coexist and even overlap. The genuine follower of Christ cannot contain the springs of living water that flow from him as they burst forth and have a ripple effect on those the believer touches in daily life. We cannot hide Jesus' presence in that way. The word *hidden* conveys the sense that something remains partially veiled. The world may see the lamp on a stand, the city on a hill, the streams of living water, and the evidence of Jesus in a believer's life without fully comprehending it (John 1:5). The full unveiling will come when Jesus' Bride, the Church, stands before him, prepared for the wedding feast. The glory of the believer is, for now, hidden, just as Christ said he went to a place where the world would not see him for a while (John 14:19).

"Hidden with Christ in God" also implies security in the ultimate hiding place. Where, in this or any universe, can one find a safer place to hide than with Christ in God? It is there he hides our true life. In this reminder, Paul encourages his readers to rise above the philosophical wrangling of culture and to find peace, inner and interpersonal. Seeing ourselves as hidden in a place of ultimate security will affect our behaviors, relationships, and emotions. We will know and demonstrate peace (Colossians 3:15).

What will change when we really believe in our true position in Christ? Do we live, day to day, as if dead to this world, in the lust of the flesh, the lust of the eyes, and the boastful pride of life? Do we see our life as hidden with Christ in God? Do we perform before men in order to receive praise from them now? Do we anchor our peace deeply in our hiding place, with Christ in God?

Rather than being ashamed of any of the answers to these questions, I encourage you to spend some quiet time meditating on this verse. Allow the Holy Spirit to guide you into the things he wants to transform, as you truly believe it with all your heart, mind, and soul. Ask him to make you aware of any obstacles and to help you cooperate in the process, in order to live in the truth of these Scriptures. Then, when God reveals hidden things, we will have some gems of beauty to place at his feet, our finish line at the end of the road home.

Reflections:

What did Paul mean here when he called his readers "dead"? Would those who know you best describe you as "dead" in this sense?

How can one's life shine as a living testimony and simultaneously hide in Christ?

What aspects of "hidden in Christ" do you live each day? Which remain elusive or mysterious?

Honestly, do you rebel at the idea of dying to this world and hiding in Christ? If so, what obstacles will you remove?

How might hiddenness in Christ and death to this world set you free in your relationships?

Prayer:

Father, thank you for the reminder that in Christ, our lives become more than the things we see and experience here. We die to the luster and lure of this world. Help me to remember this, when the world tempts me to forget. Help me to understand the true meaning of my life hidden in Christ, letting go of the need for personal glory now, and savoring the safety of your strong and loving arms. You are my hiding place and a very present help. Thank you for loving me so. In Jesus' name, Amen.

Milestone: Seeing my true life as hidden in Christ, I will live and reach out to others from a place of profound security.

Joy

Weeping may endure for the night, but joy comes in the morning. So say the Psalms. I sometimes ask myself, *What does it mean?*

Our experiences do not always line up with this couplet, do they? In my life, things worth hurting about usually do not resolve with eight hours of sleep, and the grief of some endures for years. Still, the artistic license of this piece of poetry wants to tell us something: it wants to offer us joy anchored in security and to remind us of our hiding place.

We hear a lot of talk in our culture about happiness. We consider the pursuit of it among our non-negotiable rights. Most understand happiness to mean the emotional response to favorable circumstances. If life goes well, by my standards, I am likely to feel the emotion of happiness. We have our goals, and we run movies in our heads about the way we want our life circumstances to add up. When the actual circumstances of our lives approximate or exceed our expectations, we enjoy happiness.

Happiness can manifest as a wonderful experience, but a fleeting one. The book of Proverbs says that man is born into trouble. Jesus taught his followers, "In this world you will have trouble. But take heart! I have overcome the world" (John 16:33). Today we might say, "Stuff happens, but God remains in control."

Joy, at least biblical joy, manifests itself differently. While some use the words *joy* and *happiness* interchangeably, these two states involve some contrasting elements. If happiness results from having life our way, joy comes regardless of our circumstances. Joy results from knowing that this life does not define the meaning of our existence. Contrary to popular belief, setting everything up just the way we like it does not fulfill our purpose as created beings.

Circumstances change, sometimes in an instant, and not always for what we consider the better. Those of us who follow Jesus trace our rainbow of hope and joy in the belief that he has our backs. Whatever we endure will bring about change in us that will benefit others (e.g., compassion, empathy, understanding, experience), enhance our faith (as we turn to him repeatedly), and bring about eternal changes in our character. While we may not always be happy about these circumstances, we have a joy that throws its anchor into eternity and grips the solid Rock.

Eventually, our joy finds its foundation in what we truly believe. If we believe this life to be all we have, then our happiness will depend on life's ever-changing circumstances. If we believe that what we go through on earth provides opportunities for us to lean into God, resulting in eternal rewards (in character and relationship with Christ), our joy will transcend our earthly afflictions.

This does not mean that we do not grieve, that we do not lament, or that our spirits do not cry out with groans too deep for words. It does mean that even as we weep, joy comes to us. At just the right time, we hear the Spirit whisper joy. As we embrace it, even in our pain, we move forward on the path to home.

> . . . weeping may remain for a night, but rejoicing comes in the morning. (Psalm 30:5b)

> Consider it pure joy, my brothers, whenever you face trials of many kinds, because you know that the testing of your faith develops perseverance. (James 1:2-3)

Reflections:

How would you describe the differences between happiness and joy?

When have you experienced joy in spite of circumstances? When do you wish you had?

How might unwrapping the gifts hidden in difficulties and trials lead to joy?

How will you choose joy today? How will you share joy with another?

Prayer:

I am thankful, God, that the Holy Spirit inhabits me since I have believed in Jesus. Thanks for teaching me that part of the fruit of the Spirit is joy. This joy does not depend on what is going on around me, and for that truth, I feel deeply grateful. Even in the most discouraging of circumstances, I know that you have called me your child and I have eternity with you. I have forgiveness no matter what I have done in the past. In Jesus, I have the best friend in the universe. He will never leave me or forsake me. Your patient hands will cause all things to work for my good, because you have called me into loving relationship with you and others. In Jesus' name, Amen.

Milestone: By looking to God as faithful Father, Jesus as trustworthy Friend, and the Spirit as patient Counselor, I find and share joy.

Discouragement

Some of my most downcast days happened seeking my first master's degree in seminary. The difficulties finding my joy had very little to do with the school. Other students thrived there, but I struggled with overwhelming feelings of inadequacy and anxiety. There were many days I felt so disheartened that I considered quitting. Only the original call to be there kept me going to completion—that, and a vision of a future when God might touch lives through the gifts of my training and struggle.

We've all been there. We move toward a goal with such enthusiasm and hope only to find ourselves deflated. We may continue with less-than-enthusiastic efforts or we give up completely, our illusions of immediate success now shattered.

This happens to people on so many levels. Discouragement comes in as many varieties as does hope. If we can hope for a thing, we can become discouraged about it. We recognize discouragement as an all-too-frequent stumbling block on the way home to intimacy with God and others.

The word *discourage* has two parts. The core of it is *courage* and the prefix *dis* negates it. We find similar dynamics in such words as disillusionment, disrespect and disregard. *Dis*couragement implies that we once had courage for an endeavor, and then we lost it.

We live in a culture of instant gratification and immediate fame. So-called reality programs take contestants from virtual ignorance of a skill to seeming professionalism in a matter of weeks. I even saw a gadget that promises if you buy it, your child will be an instant rock star.

Frequently in counseling, people enter the process with muted hope, eager for relief from the emotional struggles that oppress them. We start the journey together and they begin to see some progress. Then it happens . . . the setback brought on by crisis, major or minor. They often use the phrase "square one" to describe the sense that they have lost ground and now feel as if they have to start over.

Children learning a new skill, such as skiing, take it for granted that falling occurs as part of the process. Most boys swing the bat many times before they experience the reward of hearing it really connect with the ball, and there's a reason that they sell training wheels for bicycles. Immediate gratification rarely occurs when learning new skills.

However, something happens to us as we become adults. We begin to develop a sense of pride, and not necessarily in a good way. Like Adam and Eve after the fall, we become aware of our nakedness, our vulnerability. We want to hide our flaws and failures, and beating others out emerges as the big idea that drives our efforts. The idea of being bad at something, even in the process of growth and development, becomes something we want to avoid. Being better than other people becomes the desired outcome. In this derailment of grace, our efforts and perfectionism become the "legalism" (earning vs. grace) of our self-esteem. We see our value as connected directly to our last success or failure. The world supports this mentality, with the entertainment and sports industries basing themselves entirely on this scheme of things. However, we forget that lasting success rarely occurs overnight.

Grace wants to redeem us from this very scheme of beliefs. We cannot earn our salvation by our own efforts (legalism), and our value as human beings cannot be conditional on our ability to perform. In other words, we may contribute valuable things to our relationships and communities, but we have a value apart from that. The infant sleeps in perfect peace in her father's arms before she's capable of anything but existence, and a dependent existence at that. Yet the father's love for her defies description, accepting her as he does without reservation. As she learns a thousand new things, he does not condemn her for her lack of skill but encourages her with every fiber of his being. He loves her, he believes in her, and he will never give up on her.

I Corinthians 13 describes this attitude, known among Christians as "agape love." God expressed this love for us (Christ died for us) while we were still sinners, and he calls us to it in our relationships with God and others. Agape hopes all things, believes all things, never gives up, and never fails.

What would be different if we really believed in agape and gave it away extravagantly? Faith communities would put more effort into building each other up—restoring sinners gently—and would have little time or energy for gossip or rejoicing in the failures and humiliations of others. Under such conditions, people would flourish, throwing themselves freely into the feather bed of loving acceptance and encouragement (discouragement's polar opposite). We, as a people, would be an irresistible force.

Please receive this encouragement in the course of accepting *process* as the normal means of growth and change. I have a Post-it note on my music folder that says, "progress, not perfection." In our spiritual growth, we will not awaken one morning (on Earth, at least) suddenly enlightened and mature, because that kind of growth takes years, even a lifetime, to come by. But God demonstrates incredible patience in the process of bringing us to maturity. Let us embrace that process, throw ourselves headlong into his grace and agape, and share them freely with each other. In so doing, we fulfill the essence of the law of agape love: love the Lord, your God, with all your heart, with all your soul and with your entire mind, and love your neighbor as yourself. Arm in arm, as hearts knit as one, we can inspire each other to press on and overcome discouragement. Our goal remains moving in the right direction, no matter what! As we just keep moving, we make progress on the journey home.

> Jesus replied, "Love the Lord your God with all your heart and with all your soul and with all your mind . . . Love your neighbor as yourself. All the Law and Prophets hang on these two commandments." (Matthew 22:37-40)

Love is patient, love is kind. It does not envy, it does not boast, it is not proud. It is not rude, it is not self-seeking, it is not easily angered, it keeps no record of wrongs. Love does not delight in evil but rejoices with the truth. It always protects, always trusts, always hopes, always perseveres. Love never fails . . . . (I Corinthians 13:4-8a)

Reflections:

When have you felt discouraged in your Christian walk?

What do you think about the idea of setbacks as a part of many processes of growth, change, and improvement?

How might Jesus' teachings to count the cost before taking on an endeavor protect us from discouragement? (Luke 14:28-30)

What do you find most helpful when you feel discouraged? When others are discouraged, how might you respond?

Prayer:

Father, we know you never promised life would be easy. Paul and the other apostles suffered many apparent setbacks. They trusted you through difficulties to bring about the best long-term outcome for the Kingdom, which they ultimately valued above all else. By observing their lives, we see clearly that you have less concern about preserving our comfort than deepening our character, and proving your power in our weakness. Even Jesus encountered incredible opposition and suffering but ultimately prayed, "Not my will but yours be done, Father." Help me to see life not as an entitlement to have my expectations met, but as one opportunity after another to see your power made perfect in imperfect circumstances and people like me. In Jesus' name and for his glory, Amen.

Milestone: I will accept setbacks and trust that God has a plan, thus being encouraged and encouraging others.

Overcoming Obstacles

A fair-haired boy who loved the outdoors, I sunburned occasionally while growing up in the country. I remember how the nerves in my burned skin became overly responsive to the changes in temperature. The cool breeze from a fan could cause me to have goose bumps and shiver, even at 80 degrees. The morning sun might feel searing, even in the cool of the day, because my skin was more sensitive than ever before.

When burned by relationship pain and discouragement, we can develop newfound awareness and recoil from the problems that occur in them. We see each apparent failure as evidence of the things we fear: that our partner has given up on us, that our journey to find love will end in failure, and that there is the inevitability of a sad goodbye. We can too easily forsake our quest to keep moving toward intimacy.

When new obstacles threaten to block us, navigating around them on the road home becomes a matter of life and death for our relationships. When we realize that we have careened off-track, we need urgently to commit ourselves to change our hearts, listen to one another in compassion, change our ways, and seek and grant forgiveness. Just when we see progress, we may find new debris and damage on the road. Unless we can overcome these setbacks, our efforts will fail and our relationships die in spite of our good intentions.

We go for weeks, years, or sometimes decades without giving our relationships much thought. Making our way in the world, providing for our families, taking care of our homes and automobiles, and carving out a little time to enjoy the fruits of our labors leave us little time or energy to think or speak about the state of our relational connections. When we finally do awake from our denial and see things painfully and realistically, we can become hypersensitive to problems.

Most can master the skills for managing relationship obstacles. However, where do we learn them? Many couples muddle through somehow without the skills, probably because one or both of them forgive easily. A small percentage seeks professional help to learn them, and a certain percentage of professionals has competence in teaching them. We need only to look at the number of failing marriages these days to see the obscurity of these simple secrets!

When I discuss these issues with clients, I begin and end with a reminder that, in relationships, acquiring skills without a readiness to change our hearts frequently ends in failure. A willingness to try the skills, with cautious optimism, can bring about confidence and faith to believe again. Our fears diminish, our love increases, and we press down the road, arm in arm.

On the pilgrimage home, we need to remain partners. Too easily, we can drift into the role of adversaries. We have enough adversaries and obstacles along the way. Let us prove diligent to lean into one another and into God, because we can do this. It works, I promise. Nothing can stop truth when it's spoken with love. Grace and truth together offer redemption for humankind, and they can save our relationships as well.

> . . . speaking the truth in love, we will in all things grow up into him who is the Head, that is, Christ. (Ephesians 4:15)

What kind of emotional rubble tends to fall in the pathway of your intimacy with people?

What kinds of things make it hard for you to approach another person to speak truth in love?

How could you have a relationship with God, without a plan of redemption? How can we maintain relationships with people without a plan of correction? (See Ephesians 2:8-9; John 3:16; I John 4:9, 19-20.)

Prayer:

Father, thank you that when you exposed my sin to the light, you did not stop there. You offered me a way into relationship with you through faith in Jesus. True repentance and the indwelling presence of your Spirit give me assurance that you will complete in me the good things you have started. Help me to hear your voice and to follow your lead on the road to intimate relationship with you.

Help me, too, to love as you love me. If I have something against a loved one, help me to speak truth in love. Search my heart and help me ensure that you find no malice or vindictiveness there. Let your love for people flow through me as I speak truth for the betterment of relationships. Give me the heart and eyes of Jesus as I stand before my brother, sister, partner or friend. Always make me mindful of my own imperfection, prone as I am to stumble in many ways, so that I will more freely forgive. Thank you for the grace that makes connections possible and meaningful. In Jesus' name, Amen.

Milestone: I will diligently remove obstacles to trust and intimacy as quickly as they appear, whether in relationship with God or others.

Seasons

I reflect on the seasons of life, especially in the fall. Calendar photo images emerge in the usual places, and nostalgia rises. Changing colors imply impermanence: they will vanish in a week. Soon we will have to rely on our memories to relive them. Transient snowflakes wait eagerly for their seasonal dance and, depending on our perspective, offer potential as obstacles or opportunities for joy.

This is not the usual essay about the seasons of life. I do not intend to address the traditional ideas of youth as spring, middle age as autumn, and so on. Nevertheless, I find myself contemplating the many things in life that seem to have a season.

About a decade ago, I started noticing the ever-changing nature of things. My hair color began to fade to its original white. Towns and neighborhoods transformed themselves in irreverence to my memories of them. Younger relatives began to resemble full-fledged adults with growing children of their own. Even celebrities, in spite of their best efforts, showed visible evidence of another decade endured.

The word *season* can describe many things. Sports seasons, hunting seasons, and holiday seasons swirl around us in a revolving panorama. Individuals feel differently about these seasons. The ones enjoying them see them as flying by too fast. Others fear they will never end.

People, too, come and go in our lives. Priorities and shared interests parade before us in a constant state of change. Acquaintances emerge and recede as we move on to the next in an endless procession of faces. In western culture, even our family structures no longer exhibit permanence.

Ecclesiastes teaches us that virtually everything has an allotted time. What once was eventually gives way to its opposite: building up, tearing down, mourning, dancing. We cannot stop this process. At best, we can accept it and gracefully dance with its rhythm, however abrupt and unpredictable. God made us for the Garden, for faces, hearts, and places that stay forever. Therefore, change can produce an unrecognized grief in us. We yearn for something permanent. We long for Someone permanent. A silent river of sadness runs through the Eden we have lost.

Ecclesiastes instructs us to recognize the impermanent, because it also points us to the Permanent One. I think Solomon wrote to remind us that basing our happiness on the things and people around us resembles building on sand in the surf: here today, gone tomorrow.

Jesus knew people would need permanence, so he encouraged us to build on solid rock and to gather treasure that lasts forever. Hold tightly the One who never leaves. Listen to him as he says, "Look, I am with you always, even until the end of time."

There is a time for everything, and a season for every activity under heaven. (Ecclesiastes 3:1)

Do not store up for yourselves treasures on earth, where moths and rust destroy, and where thieves break in and steal. But store up for yourselves treasures in heaven, where moths and rust do not destroy, and where thieves do not break in and steal. For where your treasure is, there your heart will be also. (Matthew 6:19-21)

. . . And surely I am with you always, to the very end of the age. (Matthew 28:20b)

Reflections:

What seasons do you see at your stage of life? How do you respond to them?

How do you feel challenged by changes in life? What kinds of changes do you enjoy?

If everything in your life, including your life itself, belongs to the Lord, how should this affect the way you deal with change? How will it have an impact on your relationships?

Prayer:

Father, the truth that life drifts by like a mist evaporating in the morning light seems truer with each passing year. When I cling to the past or even the present, I feel anxiety and depression. When I can accept change as a part of the unending tapestry of life, and cling to you as the constant Weaver, I have peace, joy, and hope. Please make me aware of which point of view I choose at any given moment. Help me to choose the fruit of the Spirit and not the fruit of the flesh in relationship with you and other people. In Jesus' name, Amen.

Milestone: With Jesus' help, I will live a day at a time, letting go of the past and the future, embracing all I receive today with a grateful heart.

When He Appears

A friend of mine told me of a time when he learned a secret of mountain biking. He said that when he focused specifically on the individual obstacles on the path, he wiped out. When he learned to focus on the lodge at the end of the trail, he found that his reflexes automatically carried him around the obstacles. Keeping his eyes on the ultimate goal helped him get there.

Paul encouraged the Colossian church, whatever their changing circumstances, to keep their focus steadfastly on Jesus. He had already exhorted them to look up, where Christ sits alone at the right hand of the Father. Next, he encouraged them to look forward, to be dead to earthly things. These things cannot fulfill us long as we watch for the appearance of the Bridegroom, Christ. Our life, purpose, reason for being, and glory, exist in him. Paul explains in verse 4, that when Jesus appears, God will reveal everything with him in his glory:

> When Christ, who is your life, appears, then you
> also will appear with him in glory.

In spite of the ever-changing seasons of life, we need to see our investment in the Kingdom of God as one that's long term. Like most meaningful relationship exchanges, our relationship with

God differs from a vending machine purchase. We do not perform some ritual, say a prayer, spend time in devotions, do good deeds and immediately get something from God in return. We invest in meaningful relationships, including the one with God, slowly and steadily—planting, watering, tending, weeding, watering, weeding, etc., and eventually, when we have almost forgotten the payoff, a harvest comes. As opposed to a vending machine, our Kingdom investments more closely resemble a 401K. We keep doing the right things, even though the world and our emotions call it foolishness at times, and eventually a reward comes. It should be our hope that, as we mature, loving relationship motivates our growth and works while personal reward fades in importance.

Exactly what the reward looks like, no one knows. I realize there have been some books written of late by people who attest to going to the "other side" and returning. I even question my own apparently supernatural and emotional experiences, holding them as of secondary quality to the clarity of truth in God's Word. Even so, I think we can safely speculate about heaven so long as we are honest about that speculation.

In terms of rewards, I like the analogy of going to a concert. Let us say that a friend of mine has an extra ticket because his wife has to bail, so he invites me to go hear one of his favorite groups. He has followed the group from its earliest days, read the bios of each member, saved for the concert for a year, and looked forward to the concert for even longer. Now, at last, the day has arrived. I, on the other hand, have just recently heard of the group, so my interest is marginal and I come along for the ride. We both sit there, side by side. In every external sense of the word, we watch the same concert, but internally, we each enjoy seemingly different events because of our emotional investments.

I suspect that heaven will seem similar to this analogy. If we just "bought a ticket" and forgot about it until the day of our arrival (a debatable option), it will be far less rewarding than if we have looked up and forward throughout our lives. Look up, where Christ sits at the right hand of the Father. Look forward to the time when he will be revealed in all his glory, and we with him. There lies the true meaning and purpose of our journey on this, our road home.

> . . . when he appears, we shall be like him, for we shall see him as he is. (I John 3:2b)

How can you be certain of your readiness for Christ's appearing? (See II Timothy 4:1-2, 8; Titus 2:11-14.)

How might looking forward to his appearing have a positive impact on your life right now?

What makes it difficult for you to keep his appearing in mind?

What will you do to keep your eyes on the appearing of Jesus?

Prayer:

Father, I thank you for the certain promise of Christ's return. When he is on my mind, the things of this earth lose their luster. Honestly, too often I go around as if I'm a rat in a maze, looking down and focused on obstacles, frustrated with my lack of progress. Help me to see all things in light of the big picture. Jesus is coming, and sooner than I think. Let that certain knowledge bring positive changes in all I am and all I do for his glory. In Jesus' name, Amen.

Milestone: As I look up and forward, my motives and actions transform into those of Christ.

Legacy

Born in 1933, Sallie survived the Great Depression with her five older siblings and her hard-working mother and father. She met the love of her life, Allen, not long before he shipped out to the Korean War. They married soon after he returned, and he responded to a call to the ministry in the American Baptist Church.

Together, they had three children and ministered at several churches. She moved wherever Allen was called, and she felt honored to do it. Allen always had to work a second job to bring in money to support the family. She carried herself with such poise that we never realized the full extent of the struggles in her life. She made the girls clothes and became very skilled as a tailor. Once a year, her son would get a new pair of jeans. She stated repeatedly and clearly that though she would never have a nice house, her treasure waited in heaven and her mansion stood just over the hilltop. She diligently watched for Jesus' appearing, and this defined her.

Allen and Sallie were never famous: they never even had a large church. However, the impact of the way they walked the walk still reverberates. This writer wonders whether he would have ever heard or understood the gospel of Christ but for their reaching out to him. That was their gift, as they would witness to a stranger if prompted by God. Sallie demonstrated fierce devotion to Jesus, to Allen, and to all she loved. In her presence, we became better people, because she saw our full potential and consistently encouraged us to fulfill it. She believed in us, and she believed in Christ in us.

Affection and genuine interest flowed from Sallie like streams of living water. She always considered others as better than herself, never once suspecting that she was the very best of us. And she was. I have never known a person who so completely fulfilled I Corinthians 13. In the end, she accepted the Parkinson's that ravaged her body and mind without flinching, and did not dwell on the inevitable deterioration of her body. She always said, "If this is what God wants, so be it."

I thank God that she called me her nephew. Though I will see her again, at this moment in time, the world seems a little colder because of her absence. May each one touched by her warmth carry the torch, fight the good fight, and keep the faith—not for her, but for the One she served on her road home.

> Do not store up for yourselves treasures on earth, where moth and rust destroy, and where thieves break in and steal. But store up for yourselves treasures in heaven . . . For where your treasure is, there your heart will be also. (Matthew 6:19-21)

Love hopes all things, believes all things, never gives up, and never fails . . . so these three remain—faith, hope, and love. And the greatest of these is love. (Paraphrased from I Corinthians 13.)

Reflections:

Who has touched your life for eternity? Have you thanked God for them? Have you thanked them?

When you think of eternity and the legacy you will leave behind, how do these thoughts affect your priorities?

Philippians 2:3 says we should consider others better than us. How should this affect our relationships, testimony, and legacy?

What will you devote yourself to from now on, so that the legacy you leave will reverberate long after you pass from the earth?

Prayer:

Thank you, God, for Sallie and people like her who love you and love others, just as you have taught us. Surely their examples and the genuine love they demonstrate poke holes in my illusions about the world and what matters. They convict and inspire me.

Help me, God, to be such a person. When all is said and done, all that will have mattered will be my devotion to you and the way that influenced my relationships. The stuff I consider so important today will mean nothing. Remind me daily and help me to invest in eternity, for Christ's sake. In his name, Amen.

Milestone: I will imitate the genuine faith I have seen in others just as they have imitated Christ.

The Father's Heart

I came to Jesus as a child. Aunt Sallie took a bunch of us cousins to a summer camp in the Missouri Ozark Mountains. Aunt's greatest legacy to me was my first clear understanding that I was lost and God wanted to find me. All I needed to do was take his hand and follow his lead. Later in life, I left the Father behind for a season. He kept the vigil, watching, until he saw me coming home. These experiences reverberate when I read certain parables.

Of all the parables of Jesus, the trio of the lost coin, the lost sheep, and the prodigal son belong among the most beloved. Apparently taught back to back and in rapid-fire succession, we understand them best as part of the whole. Together they present a picture that goes beyond each by itself. The first two tell a story of redemption (seeking and saving that which is lost) from the viewpoint of the finders. In these stories, the woman and the shepherd are diligent in their search until they find that which is lost. The last of the three, the prodigal son, brings the point home because of the human frailty of the son, and Jesus' telling the story primarily from the son's point of view.

Having begun by demonstrating the heart of the father (who actively and thoroughly seeks the lost and celebrates the found),

Jesus now drives the point home. He descends from a God's-eye view (as the One seeking the lost) to territory all too familiar to us. He now looks out through the eyes of someone lost who learns to yearn for nearness with his father.

The young man enters the scene as an anti-hero. In the beginning, he exhibits little we would consider admirable except for his spirit of adventure and his devil-may-care attitude. If they made the story into a movie, a big screen bad boy would play the part. You know the type, the ones that some women notice as a guilty pleasure. They call him "nothing-but-trouble" and find that quality extremely attractive.

At the story's beginning, we discern little of the father except that he has money and property, and that he loves his son enough to give him freedom. Our wandering son also has a brother, the family hero, who demonstrates daily that he is hardworking, loyal, and dutiful. This brother emerges as everything a father could want. As a therapist, I of course wonder what it would be like to live in the shadow of such a champion. It's not hard to imagine that the prodigal might have rebelled a bit against the impossible standards set so well by his brother. We wonder, as Jesus gives us few details at the onset. The family dynamics become clearer in the final scene.

The prodigal son approaches his father and asks for his share of the inheritance *now*. Jesus does not cloak the prodigal's motives. Far from a desire to jump on an once-in-a-lifetime business opportunity, he wants to leave the region and party—literally to squander his inheritance on wine and women. The father, for reasons that remain unexplained, grants the request.

The prodigal fulfills his goals in short order. Penniless, he goes to work for a pig farmer, where he tends and feeds the pigs. The modern, non-Jewish reader misses some of the impact. Pigs, in the time of Jesus, were religiously unclean. Being near them offended Jews spiritually and emotionally, and such a job would have been considered somewhere beneath the bottom of the barrel. When hunger pangs wracked his body and he saw that the pigs ate better, the prodigal set his sights for home. He realized that working in his father's house as a servant would be better than life anywhere else.

The father watches from afar and sees the son returning from a distance, the familiar silhouette and gait finally appearing far down the road. Here, Jesus reveals the heart of the father, who does not remain aloof in his chambers. He does not communicate with his son through servants and wait until he washes away the stench of pigs and poor hygiene. Not this father! He cannot wait to reunite with his son, so he meets him on the road home.

He welcomes him, ordering his servants to wrap him in finery. In keeping with the theme of the trio of parables, he prepares a celebration. The lost son, once considered dead, has arrived at home, safe at last. The prodigal has done nothing to deserve this honor, but the father bestows it simply because of the quality of love that flows from his heart.

The other son, the family hero, feels a bit put out. For all of his dutiful devotion to the father, never has there been such a celebration in his honor. When he says as much, the father doesn't scold him but, as with the prodigal, responds from a heart full of love. "My son, my son, you are here with me always. Everything I have is yours! Come; celebrate, for my son who was dead is now alive!"

This parable abounds with possibilities. Most of us have heard more than a few applications: the nature of repentance (versus superficial confession), a systematic methodology for turning one's life around, etc. These are valid and intriguing applications, to be sure.

It seems to me that parables, including our beloved trio here, desire to teach *one* primary truth. In fact, we can get into a bit of trouble if we look too hard at the specifics of parables (e.g., not all the characters seem ethical). I suspect we misunderstand them sometimes by picking them apart, and I wonder if we lose the view of the forest by looking at the trees.

In each of these three parables, I think Jesus was trying to give his listeners a glimpse into the heart of God the Father. His heart seeks and saves that which is lost and throws a party when he finds it. Jesus reveals the heart of the Father who watches from afar and runs to meet us.

As the lost, who would not return to such a Father? Apart from him, we will find life cold and empty. Better to be a servant in his household than a prince somewhere else. Once we have truly known fellowship with him, we ultimately realize we have no place else to go.

For the dutiful among us, Jesus presents this lesson: grow a heart like that of the Father. Celebrate with him the redemption of a lost brother. Do not stand on your own works or devotion (these are only what the Father deserves), but realize he loves you because that is the very nature of the heart of the Father. Anyway, the Father sees all of us as fellow travelers and, to some extent, we are all prodigals on this path home to deeper relationship with him.

See Luke 15:11-32 for these parables.

Reflections:

What does the theme of celebration in these three parables teach us about the heart of God?

What part do the coin and pearl play in being found? What does the lost son do to reunite with the Father?

What does the lost son expect? What does the dutiful son expect? What do these answers tell you about their hearts?

Jesus' audience no doubt contained lost sons and dutiful sons. Which most closely resembles you?

In light of your answer to the last question above, what is Jesus' message to you? How can seeing yourself as a prodigal affect your attitude toward others?

Prayer:

Father, I thank you for sending the Son, the Savior and Master Teacher. In all three of his stories, there is great celebration and joy when the lost is found. Thank you for being that Father to us. If I stray, strengthen me to turn around and head home. If I value duty, help me to realize that the basis of your love for me is the quality of your love, not the quality of my devotion, and that devotion is only what you deserve. Give me your heart to seek the lost and to celebrate the found. In Jesus' name, Amen.

Milestone: I acknowledge that the heart of the Father is the force that calls me home, provides the secure foundation for abiding with him, and invites me to celebrate when the lost are found.

Drama

Drama in our relationships can take on a life of its own. The script unfolds as if written by another, and we become its mere puppets. Intelligent people lose the ability to solve everyday problems, and emotions rule. How can we find our way home to loving relationship when constantly reeling from the dramatic effects of emotional communication?

Predictable communication patterns emerge when we do what comes naturally, and that can harm our relationships. Human nature leans toward competitiveness, exhibiting itself in our communication often to the detriment of our relationships. Watch children playing and you'll see that humans want to win at each other's expense. This competitive nature, channeled constructively, brings blessings to cultures, but in its rawest forms, it destroys us. In our relationships, it presents itself as a critical spirit.

Critical messages sometimes emerge as blatant, but they are often subtle. Essentially, when we hear the word *should,* it's a potentially critical message. These messages have their place, and we would have no limits without some "should" statements. For example, we should pay our bills, show up for appointments, remain faithful in our marriages, and wear clothing when we leave the house. An excessive number of these statements, however, can make one extremely opinionated, frequently annoyed, and—even more frequently—annoying. For those of us who function from a biblical worldview, we find our standards in Scripture, especially the New Testament. When we have an excessive amount of convictions beyond those clearly spelled out in Scripture, we become dogmatic and run the risk of becoming unloving. It is because of this concern that the risen Christ tells John to write to the church of Ephesus in the Book of Revelation, to paraphrase: you work hard and teach all the right things but you have lost your first love (Revelation 2:2-4).

In a marriage or friendship, we may send the message that something has gone wrong. Of course, this needs to happen from time to time. When it happens excessively, however, the spirit of our friend or partner can begin to shrivel and die. Feeling wounded, they may react, act out in a childlike manner, and launch a counter-attack of criticism.

This perpetual dance of criticism/wounding/reaction/counter-criticism rarely takes us anywhere good. Sometimes the dance escalates into physical aggression, even among otherwise intelligent and educated people. Often, the dance results in so much pain that we retreat to our corners, bleeding and exhausted, too afraid or too tired to approach one another again. Now, our relationships enter a phase of great peril. Becoming vulnerable to affairs when sympathetic coworkers and opposite sex friends listen and provide the support and understanding people lack in their marriages, many go astray. When the criticism cycle occurs in friendships, people drift apart and find reasons to avoid each other. Christ intended something very different when he commanded his followers to love each other as God, in Christ, loves us.

If criticism resembles the *law* in relationships, the antidote, as in theology, emerges as *grace*. Agape, the relationship expression of grace, covers a multitude of transgressions, failures, and sins. I Corinthians 13 offers our most comprehensive description of agape. Among other things, it hopes all things, believes all things, never gives up, never fails, and endures forever. In the nurturing environment of agape, relationships flourish.

In helping each other to mature, *nurturing* and *coddling* are different concepts. Coddling says, "Stay a baby. I will bring you everything you need. I expect nothing of you. Don't change or grow." Nurturing says, "I love you right now, but love you too much to stand in the way of your full potential." This process of nurturing may involve some uncomfortable insight and challenge motivated by, and coupled with, agape. The pattern in New Testament passages appears as *agape/challenge/agape*. We would do well to adopt this approach as we encourage, challenge, and convince one another to press on on the journey home.

> Love is patient, love is kind. It does not envy, it
> does not boast, it is not proud. It is not rude, it is
> not self-seeking, it is not easily angered, it keeps
> no record of wrongs. (I Corinthians 13:4-5)

Reflections:

How does competitiveness influence your relationships for good and bad?

How did Jesus' teachings in the inverted Kingdom of God address striving to come out ahead of others? (Matthew 19:30)

How do Paul's teachings on agape in I Corinthians 13 affect our views of competition in relationships?

Beside competitiveness, what other sources of drama in relationships do you think of?

How will you eliminate drama in your relationships with God and people?

Prayer:

Father, after all you have done for us, forgive us for putting ourselves in first place. Help us, as Paul wrote in Philippians 2, to consider others as more important than ourselves. Help us to let go of drama as a lifestyle in our relationships, recognizing the selfishness that drives it. Assist us to reach out to you with one hand and to each other with the other, always asking, "How can I be truly helpful?" In Jesus' name and for his glory, Amen.

Milestone: I will replace my relationship drama with an orientation to grace, resulting in peace with God and others.

Holy Wars

The phrase "picking our battles" comes up often in counseling sessions. Failure to sort out our issues causes real problems. When relationships overflow with conflict and drama, any difference in perception of preference becomes an opportunity to flex our muscles and debate the issue at hand. Soon, everything, often including the proverbial kitchen sink, has been drug into the fray. Nobody wins. A week later, neither partner can remember how it started, but they both can remember the ugly wounds inflicted by the other.

Christians are not immune to such shenanigans and, frequently, we excel at them. We engage in them as Holy Wars, standing on this principle or that. Our wives should be submitting to our spiritual leadership. Your husbands should be leading the family (the way you see fit). We become legalists. The shower curtain left unclosed becomes definitive proof of the fact the spouse just does not care. We become certain that we know the dark intent behind the seemingly neutral question, "Did you water the plants?"

When it comes to this idea of picking our battles, the New Testament has a few things to say. Jesus said he brought not peace but a sword, and he warned repeatedly for his followers to be on guard. Paul and Peter, in their writings, admonish us to guard the flock, especially to be on guard against false teaching. Paul specifically warns that a time will come when people will gather about themselves teachers who will entertain them with spiritual-sounding teachings that, in the end, lack substance and truth (II Timothy 4:3). The risen Christ uses the word *tolerance* (often seen as a virtue in the post-modern Church and culture) in condemnation, warning the church in Revelation 2:20. Tolerating the infiltration of compromised teaching, he warns, will lead to the removal of his Spirit from the churches. Therefore, there is a time to take a stand and a time to draw the line.

Instead, we complain about whether the musicians tuck their hands in their pockets and the drums sound too loud, whether we have a communion table or the presence or absence of hymns. God means for us to take a stand. However, we take stands over so many of the wrong things. Non-believers listen to this and say, rightly, that they do not need it. Even they wish we had the true integrity of our convictions and would stand for the right things instead of arguing over the arrangement of the deck chairs while the Titanic sinks.

We cannot lead the world to a place where we ourselves have not gone. We need to allow the Lord to lead us to a place where very little is worth fighting about, but what is worth fighting about is worth dying for. Then, and only then, will anyone follow us. So it was with our Master.

Accept him whose faith is weak, without passing judgment on disputable matters. (Romans 14:1)

Be on your guard; stand firm in the faith; be men of courage; be strong. Do everything in love. (I Corinthians 16:13-14)

What kinds of non-essential issues get under your skin? What results have you seen when people fight over debatable things?

What Kingdom priorities are forgotten when we fail to pick our battles appropriately?

How might Jesus' law of love (Love the Lord your God; love your neighbor as yourself) help us sort out which battles to wage?

How should the fruit of the Spirit (love, joy, peace, patience, kindness, goodness, faithfulness, and self-control) influence our choices in these matters?

Prayer:

Father, I know that my tendency to attach importance to the wrong things does not please you. If I focus on superficial matters, I forget to love you. Additionally, I forget about loving people into the Kingdom. Please forgive me for the many times I have done just that.

Help me to remember what matters to you and to take a stand on these things. Even then, let me do so in love. Filled with your Spirit, let me keep the greatest commandment always before me so that I will love you and love others. In so doing, I will fulfill your will and bring people along on the way home. In Jesus' name, Amen.

Milestone: I will love God and love others so that I will stand for the right things.

Death and Life

Imagine that you accept an invitation to a friend's home. Once there, you find a house, beautifully designed and elegantly appointed. As you sit on the expensive sofa in front of the imported marble fireplace, you notice a movement out of the corner of your eye. Turning quickly, you realize it's a large, shiny rat. He perches in the middle of the coffee table, eating the appetizers. The owner of the house glances at the rat and then away, carrying on the conversation as if this were a common occurrence.

"So, is that your pet?" you ask.

"Hardly!" he replies, slightly offended.

"Then what's it doing here? And why are you letting it eat the snacks in the middle of the room?"

"Well," your friend explains patiently, as if bringing you up to speed, "it used to be so much worse. There used to be about 50 of them. Nasty little creatures they were, too. We woke up with them sniffing our faces all the time. They would bite the kids in their sleep. So, you see, we find the current situation so much more . . . manageable."

Unfortunately, we frequently take this same approach when it comes to the sin in our lives. We think that as long as our own sin seems less noticeable than before, is not a public embarrassment, or is not leaving marks others can see, we're more or less okay with managing it. Paul in Colossians 3 exhorts us, in light of our true position in Christ (alive in him, dead to this world), to put sin to death for the last time. We are not to compromise with sin, or manage it, or find a way to live with it in peaceful coexistence. We are to exterminate it.

> Put to death, therefore, whatever belongs to your earthly nature: sexual immorality, impurity, lust, evil desires and greed, which is idolatry. (Colossians 3:5)

More than a list of rules, this verse brings us to the logical and spiritual conclusion of all that lies before it and foundational to what follows. We have been raised with Christ, so we should set our minds on things above, where Christ is seated at the right hand of God. We are to set our minds on things above, Paul repeats, not earthly things, for we have died to earthly things and our true life is now hidden with Christ in God. We are not only to look up (to where he is seated by the Father), but also forward to his return, when his glory (and ours with him) will be completely revealed. Therefore, it makes perfect sense that we would exterminate sin. If we try to manage sin, it will manipulate and control us, becoming the centerpiece in our living room.

I find it a helpful practice to keep looking up and forward in my struggle to put to death the desires of my sinful nature. If my vision of *Christ with me* is clear, I am unlikely to offend him willfully, though I admit this is not impossible. If we look forward, we invest less in this world and invest more in the next. We do not indulge the earthly nature, seeking the things that last as we focus on the final destination on our pilgrimage home. Sin poses and preens as a poor counterfeit for the things that truly fulfill, the things that endure. Let us bury it and leave it there. Paul seems to believe this is possible. What would change if *we* believed it?

Reflections:

Why do you think we so easily accommodate sin in our lives, even after we are raised with Christ (Romans 7:7-26)? In what areas do you struggle with lingering sin?

How do you reconcile your accommodation of sin with Paul's command to put it to death?

How do we put sin to death? Do you see clues in this passage?

How will you eradicate the lingering sins in your life?

Prayer:

Father, I appreciate that you do not expect perfection. My righteous standing before you finds its basis in Christ alone. However, you called me to holiness, to set me apart from the muck and mire of this world. While I cannot achieve sinless perfection, I willingly hand over the areas of sin in my life that I have kept around as souvenirs of the time before I came to know you. When I think of your love for me, and when I am aware that my sinful choices break your heart, I can let go of them in order to take your hand. Help me to follow hard after you, leaving all else behind for Jesus' sake, Amen.

Milestone: With the help of God, by keeping my eyes on Jesus and my position in him, I will put lingering sin to death.

Love Shows

I remember family gatherings beneath the towering trees of Antioch Park in Kansas City. The moms laid out Midwestern cuisine on the broad rough tables and we kids descended upon the food. In our immaturity, our competition for food got tough at times. As we were not yet aware of our own selfishness, the moms had to teach us how to treat one another, lest the blessing of the feast spread out before us become the scene of a fight.

Paul felt it necessary to teach the Corinthian church about agape love, as they were arguing about the gifts of the Spirit. God's intended blessings were becoming an occasion for conflict. Let us take a fresh look at this familiar passage:

> If I speak in the tongues of men and of angels, but do not have love, I am only a resounding gong or a clanging cymbal. If I have the gift of prophecy and can fathom all mysteries and all knowledge, and if I have a faith that can move mountains, but do not have love, I am nothing. If I give all I possess to the poor and surrender my body to the flames, but have not love, I gain nothing. (I Corinthians 13:1-3)

In these verses, we see that love matters. Even ministry, service, and self-sacrifice are meaningless unless given in love. Paul goes on to describe the ways that love shows:

> Love is patient, love is kind. It does not envy, it does not boast, it is not proud. It is not rude, it is not self-seeking, it is not easily angered, it keeps no record of wrongs. Love does not delight in evil but rejoices with the truth. It always protects, always trusts, always hopes, always perseveres. Love never fails. (I Corinthians 13:4-8a)

If you want a challenge, read those verses again, and put your name where the word "love" belongs. Truthfully, there are moments that I would have a hard time reading parts of that with a straight face, testimony to the fact that we can all use more agape in our relationships. Paul goes on to say that even our spiritual gifts will one day be unnecessary, but qualities of the heart endure forever:

> And now these three remain: faith, hope and love. But the greatest of these is love. (I Corinthians 13:13)

Here is a question that has haunted me lately. If we lived according to these verses in our homes, would more than half of Christian marriages end in disillusionment and divorce? It appears that we have a disconnection between what we profess to believe and the way we live, day to day. I believe that disconnection occurs in the heart.

We may sincerely believe it, but how do we live it? How do we get there from here? If we agree that everything springs from the heart, the first question is this: Where is my heart in relationship to God? Christ has provided a way into fellowship with God the Father, not by our own righteousness, but based on *his* righteousness. Step number one is to accept his gift of salvation by placing our trust in his righteousness and not our own. This requires a heart of repentance: we have to agree with God that we have a problem. We have all fallen short of his glory, and yet he has provided a way into his family through faith in Jesus.

If we accept this, God remains willing and able to restore fellowship with himself, and gives us the indwelling of the Holy Spirit. This changes us from the inside out. He writes his standards on our hearts and empowers us to walk the walk of what we profess to believe. He changes our hearts of stone to hearts of flesh (Ezekiel 11:19).

Nevertheless, being a gentleman, God will not go where we do not welcome him. Some of the disconnection between our beliefs and behaviors happens right here. We need to welcome him into our relationships if we want to see his influence there. If we will have abundant life, we need to allow him into our lives . . . *all the way in!* This means getting into his Word, and letting it dwell in us richly, as the Apostle Paul put it (Colossians 3:16). As we read, study, and listen to the Word, asking the Holy Spirit to enlighten us, he renews our minds and we become living sacrifices, our lives no longer about getting what we want, when we want it. Agape love can then flow through us freely.

We are not the ultimate source of agape love. At best, we are fountains, but he is the Spring. As we submit to Christ as Lord, we allow him to help us love as he loved. He intends the feast spread before us to be a blessing to strengthen and encourage us on our sojourn home.

Reflections:

How do you think our culture defines love? How does culture's definition of love affect the permanence (or impermanence) of our commitments to one another?

How does the definition of love in I Corinthians 13 differ from that of our culture? How should it affect our commitments to each other?

Which parts of the description of love in this biblical passage challenge you most? Why do you think that is so?

What steps will you take to bring your love for others in line with what the Bible teaches?

Prayer:

Father, this description of love amazes me. I have heard it many times, and so have become somewhat numb to it. When I allow the Spirit to show it to me as fresh, this passage blows me away. I can see all the ways in which I fall short of this love. Clearly, loving in such a way requires supernatural assistance. Please help me to love as you love. In Jesus' name, Amen.

Milestone: By looking to the Holy Spirit and to Scripture to define love in me, I will grow in likeness to Jesus and draw others to him.

Love Listens

I have found Jesus to be the best listener ever. I can come to him with anything. Like the other sinners he loved in the Bible, he meets me where I am, loves me as I am, and believes that the Spirit will complete in me the good things he has started. Never eager to condemn or tell me my feelings are wrong, he gently reminds me of the source of my peace and keeps me moving forward on the path to maturity.

If Scripture challenges us to love as Jesus loves, listening seems a good place to begin (James 1:19). Often, when we think of communication, we focus on the words we use. While what we say is an important part of communication, we often overlook listening. Love listens.

Listening challenges us for a number of reasons. For one thing, when we listen, we let the conversation (and relationship) be about the other person. We reserve our own thoughts, opinions, and feelings and respect the thoughts, feelings, and opinions of the other person. When we listen, we engage in an unselfish act as it puts the other person first.

One of the reasons we resist listening well involves confusion about respecting another's point of view. We think that if we remain silent, the other person may think we *agree* with what they are saying. We begin thinking about being right, usually convinced that *we* are the right ones. In most arguments in relationships, "being right" is a matter of opinion. Our upbringing, personalities, and experiences often color our views on what we see as being right. The other person has their own set of ideas colored by their own set of influences. We need to be humble enough to hear them out and to love them, in spite of differing points of view.

Sometimes we struggle with listening because we view listening as a passive thing. We want to jump in with our own advice and opinions. When we do this too quickly, we actually shut down communication. I find that the other person has little interest in my advice until they feel heard and understood. As a rule, men want to fix things. Sometimes this is a strength, but when it comes to the *timing* of listening, especially in marriage, fixing too soon can cause problems. More often than not, people want us to hear and understand them. They usually have the intelligence to find their own solutions, but their emotions need expression before they can get there. Often thought of as a passive activity, *good listening is active listening.*

Active listening involves eye contact, a generally open posture, and full attention. We can tell when people are listening to us, right? It shows on the face and in the body language of the listener. Being a good listener involves nodding to show we follow what the other person says. We may say the words "I see" or "I understand what you mean." Again, this doesn't mean we necessarily agree, only that we understand what the other person is saying.

An important part of active listening comes when we respond verbally by *paraphrasing* what the other person has said. This is not the same thing as parroting what they have said. We have a parrot in our house. He mimics words I say, but that doesn't mean he understands what he has heard. When we paraphrase, we summarize the message the other person sends using our own words. This conveys understanding of the content of their conversation with us. If we get it wrong, no one gets a penalty, because the other person can tell us what they meant. Then we can be certain we understand them accurately, and they feel heard and understood.

Another important component of active listening involves reflecting the emotional content of what the other person tells us. Many men glaze over at this point, but please do not tune this out! We need to understand the gender differences of why we talk in the first place. Typically, men talk to exchange necessary information; women, in general, talk to share the emotional experience of their lives.

Therefore, men, if you desire a happy marriage, learn to listen well. This includes acknowledging the emotional content of what your wife says to you. You might say, "That sounds frustrating," or, "You seem excited!" Again, if you get it wrong, she will tell you. At least she sees you trying to hear and understand her.

Women, give the men in your life a break as they learn this skill. For many of them, learning to talk about emotions resembles learning to talk all over again. Think toddler. Others taught the men in your life not to acknowledge their feelings, and biologically, we think men have more ability to separate from their feelings. Now you're asking them to do just the opposite. It takes a very strong, secure man to be willing to go there. Be gracious and express appreciation when he tries. Teach him gently, and respect the dedication that drives him to improve in your relationship. We men already know that we're blockheads when it comes to understanding the heart of a woman. You do not need to tell us we lack insight, because this just shuts us down. Please, acknowledge our efforts and teach us to understand your hearts.

Men, be teachable, and do not judge a woman's heart for being different from yours (I Peter 3:7). Feelings are not right or wrong; they just *are*. If you listen well, your turn will come. Feelings may change as we explain ourselves to one another. However, you have to earn the right to share your own thoughts and feelings by listening well first. I encourage men to think of listening as a tool for their bag of communication skills. It should be the tool reached for *first,* not last.

In many cases, teaching couples to hear one another accurately becomes the most important part of effective marriage counseling. Countless marriages seem to arrive at a sad end because someone failed to listen. The other partner learns to live without understanding, and eventually questions the goodness of the marriage. They become vulnerable to finding a good listener of the opposite sex outside the marriage. The marriage enters extreme peril at this stage. Here is the point: listen while your partner still wants to speak to you.

Beyond listening, there are other things that contribute to communication, but listening remains essential. Two radios blaring different stations from across the room do not communicate with each other, they only send messages without hearing. As Paul said in our anchor passage, they just make noise, like resounding gongs or clanging cymbals. If we love, we listen.

> My dear brothers, take note of this: Everyone should be quick to listen, slow to speak and slow to become angry. (James 1:19)

Reflections:

What do you find most difficult about listening well?

When has listening been very important to you?

How might understanding the different motivations of men and women in talking help you in your relationships?

Why do you think James links listening and slowness to anger in the passage above?

How will you practice listening well in your relationships?

Prayer:

Father, thank you so much for being the great Listener. The Psalms give hundreds of examples of the writer venting emotions and perceptions that are not always true or mature. Yet you listened, calling David a man after your own heart. Grant me patience in listening to others to make sure they feel understood. Show me the right time and way to encourage them on, as you do me, on the road home. In Jesus' name, Amen.

Milestone: Reflecting on how Jesus listens to me, I will listen as I relate to others.

Why the Drama?

Quickly, scan your relationships. When people really get close, do you find yourself pulling back because you sense danger signals of impending conflict? Conversely, do you naively press into relationship, only to unexpectedly find yourself in the minefields of misunderstanding and conflicting expectations? How often have you walked away from churches, organizations, and acquaintances because they did not meet your expectations? True listening in relationships has encountered a mortal enemy—our penchant for drama. Certainly, drama and love cohabitate the same relationships, but not peacefully so.

Watch a group of toddlers: when left to their own devices, and drama will follow. They do not consistently exhibit cooperation or altruism. A young child functions oblivious of commandments, so how can he transgress? Selfishness emerges because he wants what he wants, when he wants it. He becomes (Freud hit the mark on this issue) "His Majesty, the Baby." We have to be *taught*, against our nature, to love one another.

Drama emerges in the very fabric of our beings. It draws some of us in as a kind of false intimacy. Others avoid it like the plague. On both extremes, it profoundly influences our lives and inhibits our intimacy.

A friend posed the question, "Why do we seem so prone to drama in our relationships?" She had read a post about drama, and found herself perplexed by this issue. We instinctively recognize the truth of the proposition, but few ponder the source.

I have to admit, the question has given me pause. Across the decades, psychology uses terminology such as *id*, *rebellious child*, and *emotional mind* to describe this tendency. Theology describes it in terms of a *sin nature*, a tendency to seek our own way at the expense of others and in contradiction to God's will. The Bible calls it sin, pride, and the way of the fool. It is not our default mode to love, so Scripture has to command a better way. The Spirit has to empower us to act differently.

The book of James would answer my friend's question thusly:

> What causes fights and quarrels among you? Don't they come from your desires that battle within you? You want something but you don't get it. You kill and covet, but you cannot have what you want. You quarrel and fight . . . . (James 4:1-2a)

You might respond, "That's not talking about me. I don't want other people's stuff." Really? The multibillion-dollar advertising industry relies on your insatiable propensity to accumulate more, counting on your lack of contentment with food, clothing, shelter, and love.

Beyond possessions, we covet status, attention, prestige, influence, popularity, power, control, and appearance, to name a few. We revel in tabloid headlines that suggest that those who have what we cannot have (fame, extraordinary beauty, and adoration) encounter misery in their lives just as we do. Envy pulsates at the heart of many sins of the tongue, including gossip and deception. There exist many different understandings of gossip, and many think it must be untrue or malicious to be called that. In my opinion, much harm has been done by sharing other people's information (even when true) without their consent. With motives being hard to identify, much gossip happens under the guise of prayer requests framed as concern. The resulting harm is the same. Among the things the Lord hates in Proverbs 6:16-19—(haughty eyes, a lying tongue, hands that shed innocent blood, a heart that devises wicked plans, feet that run rapidly to do evil, a false witness who utters lies, and one who spreads strife among brothers)—most exemplify attitudes and sins of the tongue. The other sins start with the attitude of selfishness and result in destructive actions.

Jesus responded to drama by washing the feet of the unworthy, forgiving the sinner caught in the act, and loving and praying for his enemies even as they crucified him. Chapter 2 of Philippians exhorts us to have his same attitude, to look not only to our own interests but also to the interests of others, and to submit to the Father in humility as we live among people.

By drawing closer to God through relationship with Christ, we begin to see people through his eyes. We realize the center of the universe revolves around Another, not us. His Holy Spirit within us grants us compassion and motivates us to share it. We can even have compassion for those we might otherwise hate, with his help.

Paul introduces his instructions to husbands and wives in Ephesians 5:21 with the broad command to submit to one another out of reverence for Christ. As I look beyond the face of my sometimes-troubled wife, friend, coworker, or client, I see the face of Another—always there, watching, plaintive eyes asking, "Will you honor me? Will you love as I have loved?"

Reflections:

What does the Bible say about our tendency for conflict and drama and its remedy? (James 4:1-12)

How have you seen these tendencies in your own heart and life? What results do these tendencies bring?

What does losing drama have to do with submitting to God and reverence for Christ?

What will you do to get rid of drama in your relationships?

Prayer:

Father, as I read the words of James about fights and quarrels, I recognize my heart in his description. Maybe I disguise it well, but I know its truth. I want what I do not have, whether it's material goods, talents and gifts, or great looks.

Please forgive me for lacking gratitude for what you have given me and help me to mind my own business in regards to what others receive. Help me to forgive those who have hurt me, intentionally or not, even as you love and repeatedly forgive me. Assist me to see you, waiting and watching for me to honor you by submitting to the needs of others. In Jesus' name, Amen.

Milestone: With God's help, I will recognize and eliminate the sources of relationship drama in my life by attending less to selfish desires and more to the needs of others.

Fiddle Lessons

A friend of mine in his seventies recently invited me to look at the fiddle he played in school. Like many fiddles of the early 1900s, it wears a Stradivarius label that is meant to reflect the style, not the maker. Apparently, his brother loaned it out to students and it bears the scars to show it—lots of them! More recently, it rested in a storage unit in the desert. It has cracks, scratches, and pieces of wood missing around the edges. The tuning pegs have lost their friction, and the strings hang and flop. Such instruments draw me to them. One trained or skilled in building or repairing stringed instruments could do more. Nevertheless, I love the excitement of seeing just how far some tender loving care will bring them.

Opening the case on my friend's violin, I first replace the strings. I apply some pencil graphite to the holes and pegs, put on some mid-level strings and run a bow across them. Not bad. Then I rub some dark scratch cover into the lines and cracks. Players actually esteem distressed violins because, one supposes, the woods have aged and the sound quality has reached its full potential. Time will tell if the cracks might need mending to prevent further damage. I read that restoring normal humidity can close many violin cracks, so I will try that. Lastly, I place a wooden shoulder rest (for maximum resonance) on the back. Then I enjoy the task of playing the thing, getting to know its strengths and weaknesses. What a pleasant surprise!

Now, many people have heard a poem about the master and the violin. In the poem, a man from the crowd picks up and plays a beat-up, discarded old fiddle, resulting in gasps and tears of astonished amazement. It makes the point: like the abandoned old fiddle, the master touches us and makes us sing. The poem illustrates a beautiful truth.

For me however, I think the point of my violin mending lands closer to that aspect of God that redeems and loves no matter what, that sees potential in the castaway and wants to see just how far some tender loving care will bring him. I believe he desires to manifest this part of his nature through his children as his image bearers, when we reach out to one another, expressing his love.

Whether people, relationships, or instruments, I love the challenge reaching out to the castaway. I find great fulfillment in mending the broken. If we welcome him, the Holy Spirit of Christ does his work in us and through us to bring others along on the road home.

> But he gives us more grace. That is why Scripture says: "God opposes the proud but gives grace to the humble." (James 4:6)

Reflections:

When have you done a renovation or repair of something (home, clothing, furniture, car, electronics, or instrument)?

When have you felt broken or in need of some tender loving care?

When you encounter a person who is hurting or broken, what is your response? How does your response match the heart of Jesus?

What are you willing to lose in order to gain the loving, healing perspective of Christ?

Prayer:

Father, thank you for picking me up from the rubble, scrubbing me clean, and making me better than new. Help me to walk down the path with eyes that see and ears that listen for opportunities to mend those wounded and broken relationships around me. In Jesus' name, Amen.

Milestone: I will grow a heart like that of Jesus and seek opportunities to mend broken people and relationships in his name.

New Words

As a Spanish minor in college and a Greek student in seminary, I know the power and importance of learning new words. Week after week, I would sit with a vocabulary list in front of me, covering the English equivalent until the once foreign words became a part of me. Eventually, the miracle unfolded and I could converse or read in a language comprised completely of new words. Ever motivated to mend the broken in us, Paul knew the power of new words as well.

In Colossians 3:5-6, he has just underlined the seriousness of sin in the eyes of God, highlighting those driven by the earthly nature (sexual immorality, impurity, lust, evil desires, and greed, which he called idolatry). He reminds us that because of such things, the wrath of God will come. Verse 7 seems to be a transitional statement, tying together these admonitions with those that follow in verses 8-10:

> 7) You used to walk in these ways, in the life you
> once lived. 8) But now you must rid yourself of all
> such things as these: anger, rage, malice, slander,
> and filthy language from your lips. 9) Do not lie
> to each other, since you have taken off your old
> self, with its practices 10) and have put on the new

self, which is being renewed in knowledge in the image of its Creator.

The sins of the tongue fall at the end of the list, possibly because we often bring it last into subjection under Christ. The former list (v. 5) includes sins most young Christians struggle to leave behind. Though the urges and struggles linger, most Christians overcome immoral lifestyles early in their growth, but the tongue remains a problem for many. It is a potentially fatal obstacle on the road home.

Driven by inner springs of anger, malice, and rage (selfishness, judgmental attitudes, and self-righteousness), the tongue expresses its venomous intents through such avenues as slander, vulgar language, and lies. The writer lists the sins of the tongue in the same paragraph and context as those sins generally considered as gross in the Christian community. God takes the sins of the tongue no less seriously than he does those committed by other parts of the body. Jesus taught that the content of a person's heart comes out in the words of his or her mouth (Matthew 12:34). James says that the man who controls his tongue keeps the whole body in check (James 3:2). Paul, in a rare warning to exclude a sinner from fellowship, admonishes his readers to have nothing to do with the divisive person who has been twice warned yet persists (Titus 3:10). The tongue also has great power for good, and the Spirit manifests many gifts in the tongue when we yield it to him (Romans 12; Ephesians 4; I Corinthians 13).

Those of us in the Church need to get this message. It is past time for us to leave behind the thinking that dismisses sins of the tongue as "just words." God's Word clearly states, "The tongue also is a fire, a world of evil among the parts of the body. It corrupts the whole person, sets the whole course of life on fire, and is itself set on fire by hell" (James 3:6). A spark set off by the tongue can cause more damage than a sledgehammer. It can devastate marriages, split churches, and destroy the testimony of an otherwise powerful Christian walk.

The unbeliever hears our words and dismisses Christianity as just another game people play, saying, "Why do I need the same gossip, slander, and selfishness that I find everywhere else in the world? At least most people outside the Church come from a place of directness. You see it coming. But when a Christian says, 'I love you,' then stabs you in the back, the betrayal feels much worse. Who needs it?" Even the world recognizes hypocrisy when we display it. God finds no pleasure in our praises when we use the same mouths to run one another down (James 3:9-10).

Our power to overcome the tongue lies in the same truth that sets us free from immorality (vv. 3-5). We have died to the world, to its motives and intentions. We are raised with Christ to newness of life—which includes the way we use our words. New life generates new words.

Let us submit our bodies, including our tongues, to God as living sacrifices. Please see the seriousness of this matter: eternal destinies hinge on how we use our tongues. We play with poison when we dabble in gossip. With our tongues, let us not destroy the world with venom from our hearts; rather, empowered by the Spirit, let us set the world on fire with the power of God's grace and truth.

Reflections:

Why do you think Christians struggle so with the tongue? How do we justify our misuse of this powerful tool?

How do we camouflage our true motives when we really want to gossip or hurt another person with our tongues? Do you think this fools anyone? Does it fool God?

How might seeing gossip and other sins of the tongue in the same category as immorality and murder help you in your quest for intimacy with God and others?

What actions will you take to remind yourself to use your tongue for good and not evil?

Prayer:

Father, forgive me for the times I use my tongue to spread harmful sparks in your Kingdom. I repent of setting myself up as judge and journalist in the lives of other people. Help me to run my words and actions through the filter of "Is this truly helpful?" In so doing, may I find and share deeper intimacy with you and others. Let my tongue be an instrument of your Spirit, sowing love, joy, peace, and faith. I ask it in Jesus' name and for his glory, Amen.

Milestone: With God's help, I acknowledge the power of the tongue and commit to use it for the good of his relational Kingdom.

Love and Fear

It happens about once a year. Each spring my wife announces a yard sale because the accumulation of newer things has swollen the storage capacity of our little house to the breaking point. The time has come to purge our home of things no longer needed, and possessions that have outstayed their usefulness must go. We need to cast them out. The process interests me: the new pushing out the old. I do not think of it when I bring in a new item. But in the process, we cast off the old things just the same.

One of the most surprising statements from John's epistles reads, "Perfect love casts out fear." By this, most of us immediately know that our love is not perfected. The Greek word for "perfect" here actually can mean *mature* or *complete*. Unfortunately, when we hear the word "perfect," our legalism clicks in. That is, some have used such verses to strive for personal perfection, missing the point. I have a hard time believing the Holy Spirit intended that meaning; rather, he would want us to aspire to maturity in love.

The question remains: what does love have to do with casting out our fears? When a child becomes fearful, we usually try to distract him, teaching him to count the seconds between the flash of lightening and the clap of thunder. If the number of seconds increases each time, we hear the storm moving away and we feel safe. I recognize the cognitive strategy of this method. Get him out of his fearful emotion and into his reason, and he will respond to reason. We find this rationality in Scripture. Proverbs says the way a man thinks determines how he will be, and Paul exhorts us to take every thought captive for Christ (II Corinthians 10:5) and to let our minds dwell on whatever things are good, right, pure, etc. (Philippians 4:8). Clearly, what we think about most will find expression in our lives. Beyond the cognitive exercise of "what goes in eventually comes out," what does love have to do with casting out fear?

As love matures, its focus shifts as if a camera runs, filming our lives. In the early years, the camera aims on us as the stars of our own feature. We look so cute and feel so special. When we cry, people come running. As we progress, people record the developmental milestones (birthdays, graduations, marriages, and children) as momentous occasions. Clearly, it seems all about us. We become the center of our own world, maybe even the universe.

Eventually, we realize we share the world with other people. Their cameras, scripts, and stories collide with ours—sometimes comically, sometimes tragically. Again, how we negotiate this new reality determines our success or failure in community. We can remain rigid, building walls that are high and solid, keeping others out and determining never to lose the advantage, never to be hurt. We sit behind these walls, secure in our judgments, withholding love and armed with the weapons of hatred, and prisoners of our own fears. The camera remains firmly in place.

We remain the central character, the hero (or villain) of our own story. We leave room for no one else.

Alternatively, we can turn the camera of our life story around, seeking God and focusing on the needs of others, diminishing our own importance in the process. As our concern for people increases, our fear for ourselves diminishes. I believe Paul speaks to this as he describes his contentment in any and every circumstance (Philippians 4:12). His concern that cities have the gospel and knowledge of Christ eventually outweighed his concern for his own comfort, and even his own life. His love for Christ matured so that he trusted him to have his eternal best interest at heart at all times. Growing, we too see Christ as the hero of the story. He rescues all who accept him, and we want everyone to know it. Period.

Many of us believe that we would face a firing squad for Christ. But will we *live* for him, day to day, if it means that others may disapprove of us or find us strange? What do we fear? It comes down to what we value most—the opinion of people or the opinion of Christ. When the opinion of Christ weighs more for us, we will ultimately fear nothing.

I confess I have not arrived yet. I long to . . . I strive to. I grow weary of my own excuses and am ready to step forward into a bold new world, empowered by Christ in me. Let us go there together, on the road home.

> . . . "Of all the commandments, which is the most
> important?" "The most important one" answered

Jesus, "is this: 'Hear, O Israel, the Lord our God, the Lord is one. Love the Lord your God with all your heart and with all your soul and with all your mind and with all your strength.' The second is this: 'Love your neighbor as yourself.' There is no commandment greater than these." (Mark 12:28b-31)

But perfect love drives out fear . . . . (I John 4:18)

Reflections:

When have you felt that fear dominated you?

How might maturing in love reduce or even cast fear out in your life?

How can you cultivate your love for God and people?

Prayer:

Father, the degree of fear in my life shows me I have some growing up to do. This comes as no surprise, really. I ask that you will point me in the direction of deeper and deeper relationship with you and other people. As I focus more on these, I believe that my fears will diminish and disappear. Let it be, in Jesus' name, Amen.

Milestone: As I ask the Holy Spirit to mature my love for God and others, his love will cast out fear.

Living Water

Some of my most vivid memories of basic training (a place where fear sometimes casts out love) in the South Carolina summer have to do with thirst. A mere one hundred and twenty pounds soaking wet in those days, I carried no excess nutrition or moisture on my wiry frame. The humidity left my clothes soaked more than most (an inheritance from my dad) so I literally left perspiration puddles everywhere. All that moisture poured out of me several hours a day on three-mile runs or (even worse) seventeen-mile forced marches in full gear at maximum walking speed.

Occasionally, we would come upon a clearing in the pine forests. In the middle of the clearing, would be a truck, and on the truck there would hang a large container that offered the nectar of the gods—a sweet, sugary concoction well known in those days for a smiley-faced pitcher on the paper packet. They must have bought that powder by the barrel to make that drink in those quantities, and we obsessed about drinking it. The drill instructors warned us not to chug it down, and those who did so found out why, erupting all over the forest floor. What a waste. Not to miss our opportunity, the rest of us slowly sipped our canteens of the cool, sweet liquid our bodies craved. I have never experienced such thirst before or since.

Jesus used thirst as a ready teaching aid his desert-dwelling contemporaries would understand. He promised living water that would fill his followers, water that would become streams to metaphorically flow out from them. We quickly read these passages about thirst, most of us jaded to their impact either by over-familiarity with the words or from our own sated states. Rarely do we really hunger, and almost never do we truly thirst.

Yet, we know hunger and thirst all too well on an emotional level. Somewhere deep inside, we sense something more out there and we want it! My college economics classes told me the advertising industry knows this insatiable desire in people and stands ready, willing, and skilled, promising to satisfy our thirst. You have seen the pictures of all those pretty people, faking happiness because the product they have purchased has apparently so completely filled their empty places. We look at their images, suspending our disbelief, and we sense they have something we do not. They have passed us up in the quest to fill themselves, and we see them as somehow better than us. Watch how the advertisers seduce us *without* suspending disbelief, and you will laugh aloud. Then you will cry.

All is vanity, refrains Solomon in the book of Ecclesiastes, and he would know. He had everything power and money could buy. Still, he concluded that all this only leads to emptiness. The highest number of psychotherapists per capita practice in Hollywood, California—land of the beautiful, rich and famous. If what they sell us leads to happiness, why would this be? Because what the world has to offer in the way of happiness leaves us thirsting still.

Blessed are the poor, those who are persecuted, those who mourn, and those who hunger and thirst after righteousness, counters Jesus to the propaganda of his day. You see, the deceptions remain the same, and true fulfillment lies where we least expect it. Beauty fades, stock markets fall, and skyscrapers tumble, but the love of God never fails. We need it. We have an empty place inside us, just made for him to fill.

Even when we have tasted of his goodness, we sometimes find ourselves chasing the next shiny object, substance, food, or person. You know you do. I chase mine; you chase yours. When what we have engenders gratitude to God, and we can afford it without going into debt, it can be a source of blessing. However, when it turns into the object of our obsessions, coming between him and us, it becomes salt water to our spirits, only intensifying our thirst. Then the addictive cycle kicks in. We chase the wind until we fall exhausted at his feet.

Why will we not leave behind our futile pursuits of things we cannot keep? When will we forsake the quests after things that will not fill us? Let us lay down the things that capture our attention and compete for his rightful place in our hearts. He will meet us there, hands outstretched with living water to sustain us on the road home, and forever after.

> Come, all you who are thirsty, come to the waters . . . Why spend money on what is not

bread, and your labor on what does not satisfy? Listen, listen to me . . . . (Isaiah 55:1a, 2a)

Jesus answered her, "If you knew the gift of God and who it is that asks you for a drink, you would have asked him and he would have given you living water . . . whoever drinks the water I give him will never thirst. Indeed, the water I give him will become in him a spring of water welling up to eternal life." (John 4:10, 13b)

On the last and greatest day of the Feast, Jesus stood and said in a loud voice, "If anyone is thirsty, let him come to me and drink. Whoever believes in me, as the Scripture has said, streams of living water will flow from within him." (John 7:37, 38)

As the deer pants for streams of water, so my soul pants for you, O God. (Psalm 42:1)

Reflections:

When have you been very thirsty? How can dehydration affect you?

Why do you think the Scriptures frequently use the illustration of thirst?

How have you tried to quench spiritual and emotional thirst?

How will you more consistently come to Jesus and drink?

Prayer:

Thank you, Father, for giving me the sensation of thirst so that I know when I need water. Without it, I will die. Thank you, too, for the promise of quenching my spiritual thirst. Remind me to turn to you and not the world. Let your springs of living water flow out from me and draw others to you. In Jesus' name, Amen.

Milestone: I will recognize my thirst as a need for God, turn to him alone, and share his living water with others.

Copyright Alvaro German Vilela, 2012/Used by permission
of Shutterstock.com

Stumbling

Early in my Christian walk, a lot of energy went into avoiding overt sins. You know, the big ones as defined by the local body. In the colloquial language of the Midwest, that would be "smoke and chew and . . ." you know the rest. Some people, perpetually thirsty, seem to struggle at this cycle of sin and repentance for a very long time.

At some point, we need to climb off the hamster wheel of this repeated cycle in our hearts and look around us. There are other people here. Some need to know him in his grace and truth; some need building up and encouraging on the road home to intimacy with God and others. In the Scriptures, we discover that each believer has received a gift (I say at least one) for these purposes. As we transfer our energies into serving in his name, overt sins seem to lose their attraction.

Time in the Word (God speaks to us), time in prayer (we speak to God and listen for his response), and fellowship with others (who love us enough to hold us accountable) all help us keep moving forward and protect us from the dreaded "looking back" that Jesus said makes us unworthy for service in his Kingdom.

James reminds us that we all stumble in many ways. Here he gives us a reality check in his own inimitable style, seeming to revel in reminding us (and himself) that we all fail. He wants us to humble ourselves before God, being always mindful that we dwell here as a vapor—but a Spirit empowered vapor, nonetheless.

So, if Christ covers all confessed sin, what consequences can there be? The life of David plays this out in high melodrama. God forgave David's sin with Bathsheba, and did not take his Spirit away. David remained the anointed King of Israel and went on to write scores of Spirit-inspired beautiful love songs to God, which today we call the Psalms. Scripture calls him a man after God's own heart and mentions him in the lineage of Jesus. We fully expect to see him in heaven. Nevertheless, there were consequences. The child born out of David and Bathsheba's sin died in their arms, and his children turned against one another and against him. David's own army killed his son, Absalom, as he tried to lead a rebellion to take the Kingdom of Israel from David. These consequences followed David for a lifetime, even though God forgave him for eternity.

These days, most of my sins live in my heart. More dangerous because of their hiddenness, they still carry consequences, building invisible barriers between my brothers and me. They impair full fellowship with God as well. God only knows what these sins have cost me in terms of the fullness of ministry he intended for me. Another repercussion comes in the principle, "What is in the well comes up in the bucket" (please forgive the Kansas roots). Eventually, heart sin manifests itself in the tongue, and their ripple effect undoubtedly gives others opportunity to stumble as well. This grieves God, and it grieves me.

I hope I grow (though imperfect), extending and receiving grace and truth as part of the spiritual organism known as the Body of Christ, his Church. I do not want to keep on sinning because I do not want to offend the One who loved me so much that he chose to die rather than live without me. Relationship with him is both the destination and the road home to it. By leaning into him, we will find him there, eager to say, "Well done . . . ," not because of our perfection, but because of his sustaining grace.

> . . . But when you are tempted, he will also provide you a way out so that you can stand up under it. (I Corinthians 10:13b)

> We all stumble in many ways . . . . (James 3:2a)

> If we confess our sins, he is faithful and just and will us forgive our sins and purify us from all unrighteousness. (I John 1:9)

Reflections:

In what ways are you prone to stumble spiritually?

If we could be perfect, Jesus' sacrifice would be unnecessary. Why should we strive to eliminate sin?

Do you tend to be aware of sins of the heart, mind, and attitude? How might realizing that the heart is of utmost importance to God motivate you in these areas?

How will you deal with stumbling when it happens? How will you avoid stumbling whenever possible?

Prayer:

Thank you, Father, that you are not surprised when I stumble but stand ready to forgive when I turn to you and repent. Help my love for you to motivate me to avoid stumbling, and remind me that, though forgiven, my sin brings consequences in an already wounded world. Teach me to love others so that I will not desire to sin against them. In Jesus' name, Amen.

Milestone: As I grow in love, I will avoid stumbling whenever possible, accept grace when I do stumble, and extend grace to others in the same way.

Compassion

The importance that a woman places on what she wears baffles me. Personally, from the time I get out of the shower to fully dressed takes about 15 minutes, and I do not consider myself a morning person. Imagine my surprise as a young husband, when my wife got dressed for church as many as three times because the appearance reflected in the mirror did not satisfy her! Though not a vain person, she takes care to project a Godly image that will not give men opportunity to stumble in their hearts while enhancing her considerable charms.

Apparently, how we clothe ourselves carries more importance than I realized. What we wear wraps around us, embraces us, and becomes a big part of what others see of us. We put it on and it is part of our persona. Reality shows on TV, entire programs, and many books and magazines dedicate themselves to the ideal of clothing oneself thoughtfully to project just the right image.

One assumes the Apostle Paul was not much into fashion. In his letters, he encouraged the women of certain churches to tone it down a bit so as not to cause men to stumble, and to let the beauty of the Spirit shine through them. This amounted to the sum total of his fashion advice. Nevertheless, he did talk about how we clothe ourselves in other ways.

In Colossians 3, he teaches that new life in Christ purges some behaviors and attitudes. We do away with sexual immorality, impurity, lust, evil desires, greed, and all forms of idolatry, malice, and filthy language. Pride in one's race, culture, or socio-economic standing becomes meaningless in newness of life. Christ matters supremely, and his Holy Spirit indwells every believer. Therefore, we should hold one another in the highest respect and honor. When we treat each other in a given way—well or poorly—we do so to Jesus.

Paul does move into territory that is more positive. As we eliminate these negative attitudes and behaviors, he now highlights other things we are to "put on." He instructs us to clothe ourselves in a number of things, firmly assured of our identity before God. God has chosen us, set us apart, and dearly loved us. From this sure identity, he teaches us not to take on just another form of pride, as religious people sometimes do. He exhorts us instead to show the same characteristics as the God who chose, set apart, and dearly loved us. Here, we look at the first of these characteristics, compassion:

> Therefore, as God's chosen people, holy and dearly
> loved, clothe yourselves with compassion . . . .
> (Colossians 3:12)

Paul used the word translated as compassion (*oiktirmos*) in conjunction with another word (*spanchnon*) to denote the seat of emotion, "the heart." One might translate it as, "a heart of compassion." Scholars translated *oiktirmos* as "mercies" in Romans

12:1, so the gist is that Paul encouraged the readers to clothe themselves with a heart of compassionate mercy.

One of the downsides of the attention given to the study of spiritual gifts in recent decades comes in an unfortunate tendency on the part of some to let themselves off the hook for the things not pertinent to their particular gift, a conclusion that never occurred to Paul. For example, Scripture expects the one who does not have a gift of evangelism to share the good news and teaches the one who does not have a gift of giving to give generously from the heart. So, too, Paul exhorts the one who does not necessarily have a gift of mercy to clothe himself with a heart of compassion, giving all of us the mandate to show mercy. The word differs from the Greek word (*sumpathes*) from which we get our word "sympathy." More than a feeling, *oiktirmos* denotes an attitude that leads to compassionate, merciful, and helpful acts. The merciful heart of the Father became especially evident in the active life of the Son, Jesus Christ. (See Matthew 9:36; 14:14; 15:32; 20:34.)

Please, let me challenge you to ask yourself a simple question: In any given encounter, what would I say or do differently if I were truly clothed in compassion? Might you risk being taken advantage of by the panhandler in the parking lot? Would you be more understanding with the new clerk in the store? Might you take an extra 30 minutes to shovel snow for an ailing neighbor who does not particularly like you? Would you more readily forgive someone who has betrayed you, even if they do not ask? Would your driving habits change? The Spirit can show us endless applications and implications of putting on a heart of compassion.

Compassion excludes selfishness. Compassionate people do not hold on to their resources (material, emotional, or spiritual) but share them freely. Let the dust of Jesus' sandals cover us because we follow his compassionate example so closely on this, our trek home.

> . . . The Lord is full of compassion and mercy. (James 5:11b)

> Praise be to the God and Father of our Lord Jesus Christ, the Father of compassion and the God of all comfort, who comforts us in all our troubles, so that we can comfort those in any trouble with the comfort we ourselves have received from God. For just as the sufferings of Christ flow over into our lives, so also through Christ our comfort overflows. (II Corinthians 1:3-5)

Reflections:

When have you tended to excuse yourself, saying that you are "just not compassionate"? How might Paul respond to such disclaimers?

Why do you think Paul used the analogy of clothing ourselves here?

How might the Church be different if we put thought and attention into clothing ourselves with compassion? How might we affect the world differently?

How will you make conscious decisions to wear compassion on your sleeves?

Prayer:

Thank you, Father, for your heart of compassion that looked upon my lost and sinful state and reached out to pull me up and into your arms. Help me to share the same kind of compassion with others. Assist me to be truly helpful. Let me pull people into your arms as I wear your compassion on my sleeves. In Jesus' name and for his glory, Amen.

Milestone: As I go, I will wear the compassion of God on my sleeves.

Kindness

I recently read a note from a friend who serves as a mentor to many. Her life and ministry are about meeting people where they are and encouraging them to move forward. Her note said: "My day goes so much better when I look for people I can encourage specifically." This compassionate and kind-hearted attitude has gleaned her thousands of followers. More importantly, she nurtures many of these people in their development as writers and human beings.

In Colossians 3, the Apostle Paul encourages his readers to clothe themselves in various qualities of the heart. The first was compassion, and now, we look at the second—kindness. Scholars offer several interpretations of the root word (*crestos*); such as serviceable, good, pleasant (about things), good, gracious, kind (about people). The writer here uses a derivative, (*crestotes*), which refers to goodness of the heart, and is translated as "kindness" in II Corinthians 6:6, Galatians 5:22, Ephesians 2:7, Colossians 3:12, and Titus 3:4. To the Greek reader, to whom Paul wrote, kindness carried an understanding of *good-heartedness resulting in kind actions.*

Paul's use of "clothe yourselves" does not mean to imply that we put on some exterior show, posing and preening. He does mean to say that we wrap ourselves in these qualities, put them on, and let them accompany us so that they are evident to others as we go through our days. We should take thought to what attitudes we put on each day, as with clothing.

These behaviors should not only be evident in us when others watch. Paul could have used other words for kindness in the Greek language, but he chose this one, which carries a deeper meaning of good-hearted. These kind acts emerge not merely for show (and gaining approval), but they flow from the Spirit-filled heart.

At any given moment, we make choices of the heart, maybe coming from a place of self-centered motivations. We want what we want, when we want it. We become impatient and annoyed with those who slow us down or block our progress toward our selfish goals. We clothe ourselves in selfishness. We may achieve our goals, and even have a cheering audience to drench us in approval. However, if relationship does not exist, we carry our trophies home to an empty heart.

Alternatively, we can choose goodness of heart. We can enter our days like my friend, looking for opportunities to bless others. People starve for some kindness from the heart, and notice when we do good things for them simply to bless them, without ulterior motives.

The gospel of Christ would go farther if we clothed ourselves in kindness as we go out into this world. It could care less about our dogma, until it sees goodness in our hearts. The original announcement of Jesus' birth from the angels was not a doctrinal treatise; it was a bold and open expression of God's good will toward men.

Along with compassion, clothe yourself in kindness today. Let the attitude of your heart be: "How can I be truly helpful?" The way home will be a little warmer and your Father will smile.

> . . . Clothe yourselves with . . . kindness . . . .
> (Colossians 3:12)

Reflections:

What makes kindness a rare or random occurrence these days?

When have you struggled to be kind? What was the true internal source of your struggle?

Why do you think Paul lists kindness here and other key passages, such as the fruit of the Spirit (Galatians 5:22) and in the classic description of Christian love (I Corinthians 13:4)?

How will you make sure the kindness of Christ in you is obvious to others?

Prayer:

Thank you, Lord, for making your loving kindness available to people through the ages. Thanks, too, for making it evident to me. Help me to remember that true kindness flows from you. I do not have to exhaust myself to manufacture it. If I step aside, it can flow from your Spirit to bless others. Make me aware of opportunities and empower me to do so for your glory. In Jesus' name, Amen.

Milestone: I will put my ego aside and allow the kindness of the Holy Spirit to bless others through me.

Grace and Truth

The medical community expresses great concern about the condition of your heart. Heart disease leads as the cause of death in the United States, with someone dying from a heart related problem approximately every 39 seconds. Not surprisingly, experts talk a lot about how to achieve heart health. Clearly, your heart matters. It keeps you alive!

The medical community has less concern about some other conditions of the heart, which have to do with our relationships with God and others, our emotional needs, and the lives that flow from them (Proverbs 4:23). As a counselor, I see the effects of these matters of the heart every day, and the ripple effect extends far. More than half of Christian marriages end in divorce these days. People usually understand that God wants our marriages to be kind, committed, fruitful, and fulfilling, and intellectually, we know this. Somehow, unresolved heart matters keep us from fulfilling what we believe to be right and best. Married or single, these heart matters remain crucial.

The condition of our hearts matters to God. You can find the words "heart" and "hearts" almost 800 times in the Bible. This does not include the numbers of times it talks about the *brokenhearted, disheartened, downhearted, hardhearted, heartache, heartless, kindhearted, simple-hearted, stouthearted, stubborn-hearted, and wholehearted.*

One crucial heart matter is the place we come from in our heart when we are in relationships with people. When the Apostle John wanted to tell about Jesus coming into the world, he did so from a God's-eye view. We see the two words *grace* and *truth* coupled in the first chapter of John (e.g., John 1:14). Repeatedly, he says that Christ came from heaven to dwell among us full of grace and truth. Coming from the very heart of the Father, Jesus lived and loved in grace and truth.

In a parallel teaching, Paul encouraged his readers to "speak the truth in love" (Ephesians 4:15). In doing this, he promised we would be able to grow up as the Body of Christ into his likeness. These elements of spiritual nurturance appear repeatedly: grace and truth, speaking truth in love.

By personality and in some cases by our theology, we tend to fall to one side or the other. People who hate conflict might hesitate to speak truth in love, fearing rocking the boat. Those who love a good argument and being right may focus on truth too much, wanting to be right about everything and fighting about debatable things. God sent his Son into the world with grace *and* truth because we need both. Jesus walked in this way, and as his followers, so should we.

So what does it mean to dwell together in grace and truth in relationships? It means accepting each other while encouraging one another on to maturity. It means giving grace when the other person tries to grow and do the right thing, even if they do not do it perfectly. Speaking truth in love sometimes means asking for what you need, speaking truthfully about the gaps in the relationship while remembering the relationship needs of the other person. Dwelling in grace and truth as couples also means recognizing the differences between the primary emotional needs of men and women and doing what we can to meet the emotional needs of both people (Ephesians 5:33).

It turns out that men and women essentially need different things in relationships. A woman needs unconditional love, even if she does not always act and speak in a lovable manner. This does not make her a princess, just a woman. A man needs unconditional respect, even though not all of his actions will be respectable. This does not make him an egotist, only a man. God made us different on every level. Honor the differences. Look over the shoulder of your spouse, relative, or friend the next time you are in conflict. Jesus stands there, watching, and asking, "Will you honor me?"

> The Word became flesh and made his dwelling among us. We have seen his glory, the glory of the One and Only, who came from the Father, full of grace and truth. (John 1:14)

Reflections:

The Church today rightly emphasizes the importance of grace (Ephesians 2:8-9). What do you know about the importance of truth? (See John 14:6; 18:37; 8:32.)

What parallels can you draw between grace and truth in the gospel and grace and truth in relationships?

Do you tend to lean toward grace or truth? Why?

What will you do to begin to show more balance in grace and truth in your relationships?

Prayer:

Thank you, Father, for the clarity of your word regarding grace and truth. Truth leads us to the gate and grace opens it. Forgive me if I have neglected the importance of either. In my relationships, please help me to speak truth in love so that we can all grow up as you intend. In Jesus' name, Amen.

Milestone: Speaking truth in love, we will grow into the likeness of Jesus Christ.

Fork in the Road

In Robert Frost's poem, *The Road Not Taken*, the writer comes upon two paths in the woods, and takes the one less travelled by, "and that has made all the difference." As I approach yet another birthday in my late fifties, I am increasingly aware of the implications of so many past decisions and their apparent consequences, both good and bad. In Romans 8, the Apostle Paul speaks of two paths that continually lie before us. He challenges us to walk in grace and truth and to take the path less travelled.

The paths of flesh and the Spirit lie ever before us. At times, we will find the distinction between these paths very clearly marked. Whether to study one's Bible or visit a porn site serves as an example of two paths that have distinct guideposts. One path bears the signpost marked "faithfulness," and the other "immediate gratification." A shortsighted man may be tempted to choose immediate gratification over faithfulness, but the spiritual man eventually learns to discern the destination of his choices. More often than not, the spiritual man learns to take the path of faithfulness motivated by the promised destination—peace with God and others.

At other times the two paths, of flesh and the Spirit, may be more difficult to read. When faced with these choices, both of which appear to be spiritual in nature and outcome, distinguishing between them requires a supernatural guidance system. What truly motivates us? What outcome do we honestly desire? If the answers to these questions, in our most candid moments, have to do with self-aggrandizement versus building up the Church or winning souls to Christ, the hidden nature of the path reveals itself. The path of the flesh diligently seeks to build its own ego, puffing itself up with knowledge. The path of the Spirit deflects attention to Christ, and the focus while on the path becomes how to be truly helpful in meeting the spiritual needs of another. Each of these paths may look noble enough to the outside observer but, inwardly, we know the difference, don't we?

The consequence of our choice becomes predictable as we learn from our mistakes and face the perpetual fork in the road before us. One takes us closer to our destination, home to loving and intimate relationships with God and people. The other takes us farther from that destination and ultimately merges with the most-travelled road, distant from God and indifferent to others. Be aware. Moment by moment you have a path to choose, if only in your heart. Listen to the Spirit and follow his lead. He will make your path straight.

> Enter through the narrow gate. For wide is the gate and broad is the road that leads to destruction, and many enter through it. But small is the gate and narrow the road that leads to life, and only a few find it. (Matthew 7:13-14)

Those who live according to the sinful nature have their minds set on what that nature desires; but those who live in accordance with the Spirit have their minds set on what the Spirit desires. The mind of the sinful man is death, but the mind controlled by the Spirit is life and peace; the sinful mind is hostile to God . . . Those controlled by the sinful nature cannot please God. (Romans 8:5-8)

Trust in the LORD with all your heart and lean not on your own understanding; in all your ways acknowledge him, and he will make your paths straight. (Proverbs 3:5-6)

The path of the righteous is like the first gleam of dawn, shining ever brighter till the full light of day. (Proverbs 4:18)

Reflections:

What forks in the road lie before you right now?

When have you had difficulty discerning the difference between the paths of the flesh versus the Spirit?

When have you willfully chosen the path to immediate gratification? In retrospect, where did it lead?

How can you discern flesh versus the Spirit more clearly? What will you do to make the better choice?

Prayer:

Thank you, God, for sending your Holy Spirit to live in me. He is there to speak to me, guide me, warn me, and keep me on the right path. Help me to hear his voice above all others. Assist me to obey him, because he has my best interest at heart. In my close relationships, guide me to help others to tune out all voices but yours so that we can travel home together. In Jesus' name, Amen.

Milestone: I will listen closely to the Holy Spirit and bring others with me on the road home.

Releasing

I remember when I received word about Aunt Sallie on hospice care. Down to 80 pounds, her perpetually youthful voice expressed itself as a mere whisper. Her contact with reality also transient, the new health care goal emerged—to make her as comfortable as possible until she passed. As she loosened her grip on what we call reality and life on this earth, those who loved her began the process of releasing her to the hands of the Savior she had loved and served her entire life. It was of great comfort to know that she was led by the Spirit in life and on through the valley of death.

On the other end of life's spectrum, Mary and I recently met with some beloved friends in my office at the church. Their 13-year-old daughter just received a purity ring from her parents, and they wanted a ceremony to mark the milestone as they began the process of releasing her gradually to a world of options and choices that fell beyond their direct control.

Often in life, releasing presents itself as a necessary skill. At some point, the physical misery of our aged loved ones prompts us to desire something much better for them. We earnestly want God to free them from the battered bodies that cripple and contain them. We wish to release them, no matter how sad our season of grief in the wake of their absence. As painful as the process of releasing might be, we let them go to a much better place and existence.

As parents watch their children grow in competence and trustworthiness, they transition into the acknowledgment that they can no longer control the activities and environment of the babies they raised. Eventually the ideas, values, and choices of children no longer fall under the direct control of parents. The parents' hope that the standards and beliefs they have raised their children in will hold fast and take deep, drought-proof roots. Ultimately, they have raised their children to become adults, fully functional people who can make their own decisions on many levels, whether or not the parents agree with all of them.

In my counseling practice, I remain mindful of the proverbial process of leading a horse to water. The horse, having free will, will choose to drink or not. I can offer the water in a pleasing manner, holding it still so the ripples are not frightening, and I can present it as fresh and pure as possible. Nevertheless, I must let go of the results. Each time a client leaves my office, he leaves with a prayer and best wishes for emotional and spiritual health and maturity. Nevertheless, if real change occurs, it comes because the Spirit of God and the heart of the person have agreed on a change of course. The counselor ultimately has no control over the choices of the client.

When we invest in friends, we want the best for them. Sometimes we see the course of life they take as potentially dangerous. We can warn them without condemnation and hope for the best. However, we cannot make adults (or teens for that matter) do a thing they eventually choose not to do. We must release them.

It seems I have been doing a lot of releasing lately. I hope I get better at it, but I still revert to my illusion of control from time to time. I send my writings out with good intentions, but I know they ultimately become open to millions of interpretations. Still, I must release them if they might be useful to anyone but me. I have no clear idea what God will do with them, and that's more than okay. It all belongs to him anyway, and I'm happy to be along for the adventure. Our loved ones, our musical ministry, my counseling practice, the house we call home, and our friends are just on loan to us, and God makes the ultimate calls. Jesus is trustworthy, and therein we find our peace on the road home.

God, grant me the courage to change the things I can, the serenity to accept the things I cannot, and the wisdom to know the difference. Sovereign Lord, grant that I may accept, as you did, this world as it is, and not as I would have it to be . . . . (Serenity Prayer, St. Francis of Assisi, paraphrased)

For this reason a man will leave his father and mother and be united with his wife, and they will become one flesh. (Genesis 2:24)

These twelve Jesus sent out with the following instructions . . . "I am sending you out like sheep among wolves. Therefore be as shrewd as snakes and as innocent as doves." (Matthew 10:5a, 16)

Reflections:

What kinds of things have you had to release? What things do you dread releasing in the future?

Do you find releasing easy or difficult? Why?

Scripturally, what do you own in this world? (Luke 9:58; Job 1:21; Philippians 4:11-12)

How might embracing the idea of everything belonging to God help you in the releasing process?

Prayer:

Thank you, Father, for the things you provide along the way to demonstrate your goodness. I pause now to acknowledge that everything I have is yours, to be used by you, as you see fit. Help me to hold on loosely to things, circumstances, and even people lest I worship the gift above the Giver. Come what may, help me to say as Job did, "May the name of the Lord be praised." In Jesus' name, Amen.

Milestone: I will loosen my grip on things below so that I can take hold of intimacy with God and deeply love others without worshipping them.

Humility

The Christmas Eve service at our church included a play last year. The roles represented a group of friends discussing Christmas movies and sliding in and out of characters in the movies. I want especially to mention the wardrobe here. The director asked the male and female cast members to wear black slacks, shoes, socks, and belts. Each person also wore a jewel-tone shirt of a different color. The reasoning went like this: The six of us would be moving around on the stage, changing roles quickly, and the different colors would help the audience to keep us straight. Even though we were literally changing hats and parts every few minutes, our clothing helped identify us to the audience.

Paul encouraged the Colossians to take careful thought as to the attitudes they clothed themselves in day to day. In our lives, most of us wear various hats, and whatever hat we wear, these qualities need to remain as our basic wardrobe. Being clothed in them shows the watching world that we are identified with Christ in newness of life.

When Paul wrote his letter, some in the church at Colossae followed fabricated religions that promoted such practices as self-made rules (legalism), discipline of the body (asceticism), and seeking visions (mysticism). This search led to pride in their self-centered efforts. Paul now reminded them of the one who united them, Jesus, and exhorted them to wrap themselves in the qualities of his being. One of these is pride's opposite—humility.

Humility is not (as commonly misunderstood) the practice of underestimating oneself. Speaking lowly of ourselves, I believe, is putting down God's handiwork. God created each person to be as unique as a snowflake, and this uniqueness demonstrates the exquisite beauty of a God who loves variety. People, not God, enforce the concept of a particular mold and try to force everyone into it. Scripture does not teach the concept of a perfect physical body (which changes with the decades) or the idea of a particular personality as superior. To the contrary, it clearly teaches that God sees the heart, and that's what he cares about. He chose some of the most unlikely, least-qualified people to carry out his plans. He also passed by the handsome in favor of the humble. Humble hearts see the needs of other people as more important than their own, just as Jesus modeled for us.

Humility includes knowing who we are and who we are not. The twelfth chapter of Romans says not to overestimate ourselves as individuals, because each person has a gift and a role in the Kingdom of God. We need one another. God designed the parts of the Body of Christ to be inter-dependent, with each one's role equally essential. Our model for humility is Jesus himself, who, seated at the right hand of God in heaven, humbled himself, not seeing equality with God as all-important. He became a lowly man who submitted himself to the will of God the Father, all the way to the cross (Philippians 2:5-11). These two things—knowing our identity and role, and submitting to the will of God will get us in the ballpark of humility. Becoming Christ-like as we mature spiritually will get us ever closer to home plate.

Paul has already reminded us of our identity in him: God's chosen people set apart and dearly loved. Our challenge here is to put on the humility of Christ on a daily basis, asking God to show us opportunities to serve. Our mindset: "How can I be truly helpful to others on the road home?"

> Therefore, as God's chosen people, holy and dearly loved, clothe yourselves with . . . humility . . . . (Colossians 3:12)

Reflections:

What does culture say about humility? How does culture do at living out this virtue?

How did Jesus show humility?

How does the idea of putting oneself down match up with scriptural humility?

What steps will you take to remain aware of your identity in Christ's Body (who you are; who you are not)?

Prayer:

Thank you, Father, for sending the Son and for his humble obedience that led him to the cross and beyond. Thank you for the humble Holy Spirit, who illuminates the plan of the Father and the work of the Son. Help me to know who you intended me to be, to play my part in the Body of Christ and realize my gifts are for others, not for me. Thank you as well for your deposits of grace in other people, so that I, too, am built up and carried forward on the road to intimacy with you. In Jesus' name, Amen.

Milestone: I acknowledge that I function as one of many parts in the Body of Christ, and follow his example of humility by serving others.

Patience

"Patience is a virtue" remains undoubtedly the most cliché of all cultural sayings about one's state of mind. Parents and teachers used to drill it into us as a ready reminder to chill when things move slowly (or not at all). Over the last decade or so, patience has become one of the forgotten virtues. The marketing of instant-everything from soup to messaging has implied impatience into our lives. We complain when road construction causes us to drive a few blocks out of our way, forgetting that many people in the world would consider an automobile ride an extreme luxury.

In addition to compassion, kindness, humility, and gentleness, the Apostle Paul encourages us to clothe ourselves in patience. It seems that the success of the other qualities depends on our ability to hang in there when progress seems slow to nonexistent. The rest accomplish little unless we stay ready to endure the sometimes-tedious process of spiritual growth, as we encouraging one another on toward maturity.

In Scripture, patience weaves its way into some of the most significant listings, including the fruit of the spirit (Galatians 5) and the evidence of agape love (I Corinthians 13). Its presence demonstrates our sanctification (as it goes against our selfish human nature), and shows to those around us the presence of the Holy Spirit within us. As his agape does its work within, it flows out of us onto and into others . . . if we clothe ourselves in patience.

Several years ago, our little town began to exhibit growth, and not all of it was convenient. The days of being able to accomplish three errands in thirty minutes disappeared. I found myself feeling impatient when store personnel seemed slow or unresponsive, talking to their friends as opposed to moving customers on through the line. However, I felt convicted that if I acted like a jerk on Thursday (for example) and praised God on the platform on Sunday, I might cause people to stumble. They would be right to expect that my professed belief in God should call out better things in me than fleshly impatience. Therefore, I asked God to help me with this for the sake of the Name.

First, I did what I could to set realistic goals. Taking into account the fact that more people equal more traffic and lines at the checkout, I decided not to try to run an errand in less than 45 minutes. If things went smoothly, I could squeeze in a second errand. I now consider that extra accomplishment a luxury, not an entitlement. I also tried to adjust my thinking from selfishness (e.g., *these people need to get out of my way and stop slowing me down*) to compassion and relationship. Such questions as these replaced selfish thoughts: What if the other person is doing their best? What might they be going through in their lives today? How can I offer them Jesus in a meaningful way right here and now? What can I learn from their lack of urgency? What qualities does God want to teach me through these circumstances? How can I be a living sacrifice in this circumstance? What would God do with me if I could let go of impatience? Truthfully, we can find countless ways of viewing a single situation, producing countless possible emotional responses.

These thoughts keep me busy while I wait in line. My mind unclenches and I remember not to sweat the small stuff. I consider people, even those I do not know, more important than my personal goals and timelines. Since I have combined these practices (outer choices, prayer, and inner perspective), many people have thanked me for showing patience. It does not come from me, but it is becoming a part of me as Christ transforms me and clothes me in his Spirit . . . another crucial step along the way on the path home to intimacy.

> Therefore, as God's chosen people, holy and dearly
> loved, clothe yourselves with . . . patience . . . .
> (Colossians 3:12)

> But the fruit of the Spirit is love, joy, peace,
> patience . . . . (Galatians 5:22)

> Therefore, I urge you, brothers, in view of God's
> mercy, to offer your bodies as living sacrifices,
> holy and pleasing to God—this is your spiritual
> act of worship. Do not conform any longer to the
> pattern of this world, but be transformed by the
> renewing of your mind. Then you will be able to

test and approve what God's will is—his good, pleasing and perfect will. (Romans 12:1-2)

Submit to one another out of reverence for Christ. (Ephesians 5:21)

Reflections:

How does culture nurture impatience in us? Why?

How can impatience hinder our intimacy with God? With others?

How could patience help us in our quest for all other virtues?

How might the patience of Christ, flowing through us, help others on their journey to intimacy with God and others?

Prayer:

Father, I am reminded of the familiar joke, "Give me patience—now!" In Scripture, we see that things rarely happen this way. The cultivation of patience requires patience. Left to our own devices, we remain caught in an endless loop, like the person who cannot land a job due to lack of work experience. I am thankful that you do not leave us alone in the struggle for patience.

Help me to lay aside my ego and let your Holy Spirit cultivate patience in me. I know that for this to happen, I need to think more about you (and others) and less about me. Please remind me to listen to your voice as you encourage me to exhibit the patience of Jesus in my daily walk. Bless others with your patience through me, just as you have blessed me with your incredible patience time after time. In Jesus' name, Amen.

Milestone: As the Holy Spirit opens my eyes to the needs of others, I exhibit the patience of Jesus.

Grateful Hearts

When we go to Nashville for Christian counseling conferences, we stay at the elegant hotel that hosts the conference. Growing up, both Mary and I had blue-collar, simple homes, where rooms and fixtures were functional. By contrast, the Nashville hotel astounds us. We try not to be too obvious in our astonishment, but our hearts brim with gratitude. As I look about at the 7,000 guests, I sometimes wonder whether other people's observations of the hotel are the same. The perceptions of the heart color every experience.

Paul has just laid a foundation of the Colossian church's identity in newness of life in Christ, having exhorted them to leave behind those things that will call down the wrath of God. Reminding them to wear the qualities of the Spirit on their sleeves, and to teach and admonish the church through any and every means, including music, Paul now addresses their motivation: they are to do this with gratitude in their hearts.

> Let the word of Christ dwell among you richly as you teach and admonish one another with all wisdom, and as you sing psalms, hymns and spiritual songs with gratitude in your hearts to God. (Colossians 3:16)

The close linking of this phrase to the musical themes in the same sentence implies that gratitude needs to be at the center of our music (in its varied forms), even as we use it to teach each other the mysteries of God. The previous paragraphs demonstrate that readers can thank God for many things. They have been raised from spiritual death to newness of life; the peace of Christ now can rule in their hearts; they can now clothe themselves in such Holy Spirit qualities as compassion, kindness, humility, gentleness, and patience. Earlier, Paul added the brief sentence "And be thankful" (vs. 15), linking it to peace in the Body of Christ.

So many things loop through gratitude: peace with God and others, devoted service, and generosity of spirit. Gratitude motivates a multitude of virtues and washes away our resentments. Resentment arises from not getting what we believe we deserve, whether from God or people. Gratitude neutralizes resentment because in it, we acknowledge that we do not deserve what we already have: we have become God's chosen people, holy (set apart) and dearly loved (vs. 12).

Would those who know you intimately describe your heart as grateful? As you look into your heart today, asking the Spirit to illuminate it, what do you find there? Do you see harbored resentments about the things you feel entitled to but do not have? Will you discover nurtured gratitude for the grace God has extended to you, resulting in rivers of living water that splash on those around you? We stand at another fork in the road. Choose the path that leads to peace and blessing. We have taken the other path long enough: we already know where it leads. Press on. Do not look back. And be grateful.

> Let the peace of Christ rule in your hearts, since as members of one Body you were called to peace. And be thankful. (Colossians 3:15)

Reflections:

What kinds of spiritual and emotional qualities result from gratitude? What behaviors follow when we are grateful?

When you think of times when you lacked peace, how would you now rate your gratitude at those times?

Why does Paul have to remind us to have grateful hearts?

How will you feed gratitude (and starve its opposites)? How will deeper gratitude affect your relationships?

Prayer:

Father, just now, I want to come before you asking nothing. I simply want to thank you for all you have given me. If I had what I truly deserve, I would be without peace now and without hope for eternity. I lay my weary head on the knee of Jesus, thankful to be his friend. I pray in his name and for his glory, Amen.

Milestone: As I think of the many gifts God gives, my heart fills with the gratitude and peace that will enhance my relationships with God and others.

The Sign above the Door

On a recent day trip to a resort town, Mary and I were wandering through some backstreets along the way. We happened upon a beautifully decorated door, gilded with leaves and vines of semi-precious metals. Above the door, a sign read:

Members Only

The meaning was clear: You are not welcome here unless you are somehow elite. Presumably, you are not qualified. Distinctions made, artificial boundaries are enforced.

The third chapter of Paul's letter to the Colossians contains a call to grateful unity in spite of cultural distinctions and traditional prejudices:

Here there is no Greek or Jew, circumcised or uncircumcised, barbarian, Scythian, slave or free, but Christ is all, and is in all. (Colossians 3:11)

Today's reader misses the impact of Paul's statements unless he or she understands the distinctions to which the writer refers. The racial and cultural differences between the groups mentioned stood light years apart. Paul himself was reared in the Jewish tradition that considered Jews God's darlings and considered gentiles (often referred to in the general category of Greeks) to be "dogs." The reference to circumcised (Jews) versus uncircumcised (gentiles) seems a reiteration, but it had clear meaning within the early Church as some (including the Apostle Peter early on) felt that those coming to Christ needed to be circumcised to become part of the family of God. Ouch. Paul asserts here that God has no chosen race, and no distinction needed to be made to separate one people from another (the lineage of the Messiah now accomplished). The Jews did not hold the only exclusivist ideas. By saying "no barbarian", Paul reminds the Greeks that their pride held no validity either. "Barbarian" meant any person who did not speak Greek, generally thought of in those days as being uncivilized. Similarly, Scythians had the reputation of being little better than savage beasts, and were thought of as brutes. Society called slaves and free people the "owned" (property) and the "owner."

Today, we might say "duh" to such distinctions, finding them backwards and primitive. Yet in this country, we have owned each other and dominated races that got in the way of the manifestation of what we believed to be our destiny. I have counseled minorities who bore testimony that prejudice still thrives, and they spoke not of such debatable things as job promotions. I know people who live in fear right now because they were born into a minority race. We pigeonhole one another based on other so-called differences, such as education, upbringing, regions of the country, and socio-economic prejudices that run both ways. I commonly hear people characterize local bodies of Christ based on stereotypes of the people who go there. In my own community, we may talk about a certain church being the "farmer's church," the "cool church," or a "yuppie church." When such distinctions create false barriers that God never intended, we can careen off-track. God does not see such distinctions or, if he does, he enjoys the diversity of people and does not value one over the other.

Of course, *diversity* can be taken too far, implying there are no rights or wrongs anymore. That was not Paul's message, and it is not mine. The divisions God hates includes those by which one social group judges and looks down upon, even dehumanizes, another in order to feel superior. When we do this in God's name, God help us!

The old saying, "The ground is level at the foot of the cross," still rings true. No group of people stands superior in God's sight to another. No one individual can boast of being better than anyone else, though some have strengths or talents that bring them more recognition and praise from other people. It took the same sacrifice for sins for each of us. God considers the role of each as equally essential to the Body of Christ. If God welcomes all so inclusively, so should we. God has invited everyone to the banquet. Christ's Kingdom is not a country club. Above the door to our home in God the sign reads clearly:

Christ is all, and in all.

Reflections:

Why do you think people tend to pigeonhole one another? List some pigeonholes you have heard (or used):

What does Paul teach about divisions among people in the Kingdom of Christ?

What resistance do you feel to giving up your pigeonholes?

How will you erase the artificial boundaries that you use to set yourself apart from other believers?

Prayer:

Thank you, Father, that the sign above the gate makes allowance for me. Help me to see others as more important than myself. I join my brothers and sisters of all colors and classes, on my knees before the throne of Christ. For his glory, Amen.

Milestone: On my knees before Jesus, I will eliminate all artificial boundaries between others and me.

Endurance

How many glittering dreams and visions have we run after only to find ourselves bent over with pain, holding our sides and afraid to run again? That career goal we wanted to achieve, the Bible class we wanted to teach, that program we wanted to champion, that spiritual discipline we wanted to own—whatever the dreams or visions, we have seen them lose their luster as we lost our passion. In some circumstances, just following Christ can seem impossible. In the United States, we face a (mostly) friendly attack. Rather than full on forbiddance of gathering to praise Jesus, western culture offers millions of distractions . . . and more by the minute. In some other countries, a harsher attack is under way. Some of you reading this may be doing so in secret, hoping for a glimpse of Jesus or a nourishing fragment from his Word, risking persecution or death. All artificial distinctions aside, our race toward home is the same one, and we run it together.

Sometimes we stand there, holding our painful metaphorical sides from the exertion, and we ask, "What's the use?" After all, we have bills to pay, human relationships to maintain, so-called *real* responsibilities in the material world. Who has time or energy to grow in their faith and commitment to Christ? We have been saved by faith—surely, that's enough!

When Jesus wanted to teach deep theological truths, he turned for enduring examples to the world around him. So, when he wanted to teach the importance of finishing strong, Jesus talked about sowing seeds. Some fall along the path, exposed, and birds eat some. Some seeds fall on rocky soil and the plants, which seem to flourish at first, wither and die in the heat of the sun. Weeds strangle some seedlings. A certain percentage actually takes deep root and bears the intended crop. We can learn some things about endurance from this story about seeds.

Of course, the seed is the Word of God. It is truth, the gospel, the written and spoken mind of Christ, or at least what we need of it to get through this life intact while blessing others. We people resemble the soil. If we fail to understand the truths of the Kingdom, they leave us. In other words, some people reject the Word. No tender inroad exists for the Word to take root deeply. Some seem to enter the Kingdom with a flourish and hold out great promise as followers of Christ and potential leaders of flocks of the Lord. However, they do not fully embrace the Word: the roots remain shallow and they fall away when persecution comes because of the Word. Still other people seem to have the right kind of tender hearts for the Word to penetrate and take root, but the cares of the world (worries or wealth) come in and strangle the life from them.

As I look back over my life, I realize I have resembled all of those kinds of soil. At times, my heart has been like the path—lacking understanding—and I have missed the truth Jesus wanted to give me. At other times, I most closely resembled the shallow soil—lots of panache but not much depth. To those who loved me, it might have appeared that at times I had fallen away. These days, the cares of the world weigh heavily upon me, and I hear thousands of them as a professional counselor. Practical concerns keep plodding forward, no matter what emotional struggle I may be dealing with. Worries and concerns can all but strangle my joy, if I let them.

God means for us to live as the deep and tender soil that takes the Word to heart and keeps threats far from our strong-rooted grasp on him. We are ruined for all but him, and nothing else will do. We clearly see the shams of the world. The two deceivers, victory and defeat, do not distract us. We persevere with our eyes fixed on him.

How does he find your heart today? Does he find there a soft spot he can enter? There stands only One we can depend upon come rain or sunshine, flood or drought. On the best day of your life, he is there, beaming from ear to ear to see his friend so happy. On the hardest day of your life, he is present as well, compassionately understanding that evil has entered the world and that you deal with some of its consequences. He patiently waits to redeem it all, at the right time.

I do not know what threatens to sideline you today. Maybe you feel abused or abandoned, or both. Perhaps the glittering promises of the world entice you. You might face a grief that feels like slow amputation without anesthesia. Maybe you read this at peril of imprisonment or even death. I do not know . . . but Jesus does.

In relationship with one another, as we let people in and become a part of faith fellowships like a local church, we can sometimes be the voice of Jesus to each other, cheering each other on. The book of Hebrews uses the metaphor of the spiritual life as a race, exhorting us to finish strong, and encourage one another on, staying in fellowship and keeping our eyes on the finish line together.

You run your race on the tracks of integrity, faithfulness, and relationships. Jesus stands at the finish line with arms open wide, face beaming with joy, cheering you on. If you listen to his teachings and run the race his way, your joy will be full: God will challenge and bless you, and you will receive the ultimate medal at the end of the race, with Jesus' words:

> Well done, my good and faithful servant. Come
> and enter your Master's happiness!

> See the Parable of the Sower. (Matthew 13:3-9:
> Mark 4:3-9)

> . . . let us throw off everything that hinders and
> the sin that so easily entangles, and let us run with
> perseverance the race marked out for us. Let us
> fix our eyes on Jesus, the author and perfecter of
> our faith, who for the joy set before him endured
> the cross, scorning its shame, and sat down at the
> right hand of the throne of God. Consider him

who endured such opposition from sinful men, so that you will not grow weary and lose heart. (Hebrews 12:1-3)

Let us not become weary in doing good, for at the proper time we will reap a harvest if we do not give up. (Galatians 6:9)

You have persevered and have endured hardships for my name, and have not grown weary. (Revelation 2:3)

Reflections:

What are some things that threaten to sideline your journey to intimacy with God and others?

Are you more aware of hard attacks or friendly attacks to your faithfulness?

If you have strayed from the path, what do you need to do to return? (I John 1:9)

According to the Hebrews passage above, how can you be sure of finishing strong?

Prayer:

Thank you, Father, for your compassion and faithfulness to me. Though you may bless me here, help me to remember this world is not my ultimate destination. By the undying tenderness of your Holy Spirit, keep on calling me home and find me faithful on the road. In Jesus' name, Amen.

Milestone: Keeping my eyes upon Jesus, I will bring others with me as I finish strong on the journey home.

Copyright Kenneth Sponsler, 2012/ Used by permission
from Shutterstock.com

Benediction

Father, everything I have belongs to you: Please use it or not, in your timing and not mine. I trust that you have the best interest of your Kingdom, and me as a part of it, at heart at all times. I do not presume to counsel you but merely ask that you motivate and guide me to offer my gifts at the right time and place. The rest, I acknowledge, remains beyond my control, because you are God and I, thankfully, am not. In Jesus' name, Amen.